IBM SPSS Modeler Essentials

Effective techniques for building powerful data mining and predictive analytics solutions

Jesus Salcedo
Keith McCormick

BIRMINGHAM - MUMBAI

IBM SPSS Modeler Essentials

First published: December 2017

Production reference: 1211217

Published by Packt Publishing Ltd.
Livery Place
35 Livery Street
Birmingham
B3 2PB, UK.

ISBN 978-1-78829-111-8

www.packtpub.com

Credits

Authors
Jesus Salcedo
Keith McCormick

Reviewer
Bowen Wei

Commissioning Editor
Amey Varangaonkar

Acquisition Editor
Chandan Kumar

Content Development Editor
Trusha Shriyan

Technical Editor
Jovita Alva

Copy Editor
Safis Editing

Project Coordinator
Kinjal Bari

Proofreader
Safis Editing

Indexer
Rekha Nair

Graphics
Tania Dutta

Production Coordinator
Aparna Bhagat

About the Authors

Jesus Salcedo has a PhD in psychometrics from Fordham University. He is an independent statistical consultant and has been using SPSS products for over 20 years. He is a former SPSS curriculum team lead and senior education specialist who has written numerous SPSS training courses and has trained thousands of users.

Keith McCormick is an independent data miner, trainer, conference speaker, and author. He has been using statistical software tools since the early 90s, and has been conducting training since 1997. He has been data mining and using IBM SPSS Modeler since its arrival in North America in the late 90s. He is also an expert in other packages of IBM's SPSS software suite, including IBM SPSS statistics, AMOS, and text mining. He blogs and reviews related books as well.

About the Reviewer

Bowen Wei is a senior software engineer and data scientist at IBM IoT Analytics.

He focuses on predictive asset maintenance, visual inspection, and deep learning. He is the lead in the data science team and IoT analytic solution team. He is currently doing research in the abnormal detection and deep learning image classification areas.
He joined the IBM SPSS Modeler development team in 2010 and was transferred to the analytic solution team in 2013.

www.PacktPub.com

For support files and downloads related to your book, please visit www.PacktPub.com. Did you know that Packt offers eBook versions of every book published, with PDF and ePub files available? You can upgrade to the eBook version at www.PacktPub.com and as a print book customer, you are entitled to a discount on the eBook copy. Get in touch with us at service@packtpub.com for more details. At www.PacktPub.com, you can also read a collection of free technical articles, sign up for a range of free newsletters and receive exclusive discounts and offers on Packt books and eBooks.

https://www.packtpub.com/mapt

Get the most in-demand software skills with Mapt. Mapt gives you full access to all Packt books and video courses, as well as industry-leading tools to help you plan your personal development and advance your career.

Why subscribe?

- Fully searchable across every book published by Packt
- Copy and paste, print, and bookmark content
- On demand and accessible via a web browser

Customer Feedback

Thanks for purchasing this Packt book. At Packt, quality is at the heart of our editorial process. To help us improve, please leave us an honest review on this book's Amazon page at `https://www.amazon.com/dp/1788291115`. If you'd like to join our team of regular reviewers, you can email us at `customerreviews@packtpub.com`. We award our regular reviewers with free eBooks and videos in exchange for their valuable feedback. Help us be relentless in improving our products!

To my beautiful Blue, I could not have done this without you. Thank you.

-Jesus

Table of Contents

Preface

We are proud to present this intentionally short book on the essentials of using IBM SPSS Modeler. Data science and predictive analytics are hot topics right now, and this book might be perceived as being inspired by these new and exciting trends. While we certainly hope to attract a variety of readers, including young practitioners that are new to the field, in actuality the contents of this book have been shaped by a variety of forces that have been unfolding over a period of approximately 25 years.

In 1992, Colin Shearer and his colleagues, then at ISL, were finding, as Colin himself described it, that *data mining projects involved a lot of hard work, and that most of that work was boring*. Specifically, to get to the rewarding tasks of finding patterns using the modeling algorithms you had to do a lot of repetitive preparatory work. It was this observation—that virtually all data mining projects share some of the same routine operations—that gave birth to the idea of the first data mining workbench, Clementine (now called IBM SPSS Modeler). The software was designed to make the repetitive tasks as quick and easy as possible. It is that same observation that is at the heart of this book. We have carefully chosen those tasks that apply to nearly all Modeler projects. For that reason, this book is decidedly not encyclopedic, and we sincerely hope that you can outgrow this book in short order and can then move on to more advanced features of Modeler and explore its powerful collection of features.

Another inspiration for this book is the history of Clementine documentation and training from the early 1990s to the present. Given the motivation behind the software, early documentation often focused on short, simple examples that could be carefully followed and then imitated in real-world examples, even though the real-world applications were always much more complex. Some of the earliest examples of this were the original **Clementine Application Templates** (**ISL CATs**) from the 1990s, which have evolved so much as to be unrecognizable.

The two of us first encountered Modeler as members of the SPSS community in the period between SPSS's acquisition of ISL (1998) and IBM's acquisition of SPSS (2009). We were both extensively involved in Modeler training for SPSS. Jesus was the training curriculum lead for IBM SPSS at one point after the acquisition. It soon became clear that training in Modeler was going to evolve after the acquisition and more and more entities were going to be involved in training. Some years later, we found ourselves working together at an IBM partner and built a complete SPSS Statistics and SPSS Modeler curriculum for that company. We have spent hundreds of hours discussing Modeler training and thousands of hours conducting Modeler training. We are passionate about how to create the ideal experience for new users of Modeler. We anticipate that the readers of this book will be brand new users engaged in self-study, students in classes that use Modeler, or participants in short courses and seminars such as the ones that we have taught for years.

In 2010, also in response to the changing marketplace after the IBM acquisition, Tom Khabaza (data mining pioneer and one of the earliest members of the ISL/Clementine team) and Keith started a dialog about a possible rookie book about SPSS Modeler. We knew that Modeler might be reaching new audiences. We had spirited discussions and produced a detailed outline, but the project never quite got off the ground. In 2011, without any knowledge of our beginner's guide concept, Packt reached out to Keith and wanted him to recruit others to write a more advanced Modeler book in a cookbook format. At first, Tom and Keith resisted because we thought that a beginner's guide was badly needed and we had an existing plan. However, it all worked out in the end. We combined forces with almost a dozen Modeler experts, including Colin Shearer, who kindly wrote the foreword. Jesus and other experts we knew joined as either co-authors or technical reviewers. The success of the *IBM SPSS Modeler Cookbook* (2013) demonstrated that more advanced content was also needed.

This book would have been completely different if it had been written before the cookbook. Knowing that the cookbook exists has allowed us to stick to our goal of writing a quick and easy read with only the absolute essentials. It has been designed to dovetail nicely with the cookbook and serve as a kind of prequel. In designing this book, we were quite consciously aware that many people who read this book might use our *IBM SPSS Modeler Essentials Packt* video course as a companion. Since we tried to prioritize the absolute essentials in both, they necessarily cover similar ground. However, we chose different case study datasets for each, precisely to support the kind of learning that would come from working through both. We truly believe that they complement each other.

In that spirit, we have chosen a single case study to use throughout the book. It is just complex enough to suit our purposes, but clearly falls short of the complexity of a real-world example. This is a conscious decision. Work through this book. It is designed to be an experience, and not just a read, so follow it step by step from cover to cover. While we hope this book may also be useful to refer to later, we are trying to craft a positive (and easy) first-time experience with Modeler. Also, although we offer a sufficiently complex dataset to show the essentials, we do not attempt to fashion an elaborate scenario to place the dataset into a business context. This is also a conscious decision. We felt that a book on the essentials of Modeler should be a much more *point and click* book than a theory book. So if you want a book that emphasizes theory over practice, this may not be the best choice to begin your journey. We do rehearse the basic steps behind how modeling works in Modeler, but given the book's length, there is simply no room to discuss all the algorithms and the theory behind them in this book. We spend virtually all of the book pages on Data Understanding, Data Preparation, Modeling and Model Assessment, and spend virtually no pages on Business Understanding, Business Evaluation, and Deployment. Having said that, we care deeply about helping the reader understand why they are performing each step, and will always place the *point and click* steps in a proper context. That is why we are so carefully selective about how many steps, and which steps, we include in this short book.

IBM SPSS Modeler enables you to explore data, identify important relationships that you can leverage, and build predictive models quickly, allowing your organization to base its decisions purely on the insights obtained from your data. It is our hope that you enjoy mining your data with Modeler and that this book serves as your guide to get you started on this journey. We sincerely hope that you enjoy learning from this book as much as we have enjoyed teaching its content.

What this book covers

Chapter 1, *Introduction to Data Mining*, introduces the notion of data mining and the CRISP-DM process model. You will learn what data mining is, why you would want to use it, and some of the types of questions you could answer with data mining.

Chapter 2, *The Basics of Using IBM SPSS Modeler*, introduces the Modeler graphic user interface. You will learn where different components of the program are located, how to work with nodes and create streams, and how to use various help options.

Chapter 3, *Importing Data into Modeler,* introduces the general data structure that is used in Modeler. You will learn how to read and display data, and you will be introduced to the concepts of measurement level and field roles.

Chapter 4, *Data Quality and Exploration*, focuses on the Data Understanding phase of data mining. We will spend some time exploring our data and assessing its quality. This chapter introduces the Data Audit node, which is used to explore and assess data. You will see this node's options and learn how to look over its results. You will also be introduced to the concept of missing data and will be shown ways to address it.

Chapter 5, *Cleaning and Selecting Data*, introduces the Data Preparation phase, so we can fix some of the problems that were previously identified during the Data Understanding phase. You will be shown how to select the appropriate cases for analysis, how to sort cases to get a better feel for the data, how to identify and remove duplicate cases, and how to reclassify categorical values to address various types of issues.

Chapter 6, *Combining Data Files*, continues with the Data Preparation phase of data mining by filtering fields and combining different types of data files.

Chapter 7, *Deriving New Fields*, introduces the Derive node. The Derive node can perform different types of calculations so that users can extract more information from the data. These additional fields can then provide insights that may not have been apparent. In this chapter, you will learn that the Derive node can create fields as formulas, flags, nominals, or conditionals.

Chapter 8, *Looking for Relationships between Fields*, focuses on discovering simple relationships between an outcome variable and a predictor variable. You will learn how to use several statistical and graphing nodes to determine which fields are related to each other. Specifically, you will learn to use the Distribution and Matrix nodes to assess the relationship between two categorical variables. You will also learn how to use the Histogram and Means nodes to identify the relationship between categorical and continuous fields. Finally, you will be introduced to the Plot and Statistics nodes to investigate relationships between continuous fields.

Chapter 9, *Introduction to Modeling Options in IBM SPSS Modeler*, introduces the different types of models available in Modeler and then provides an overview of the predictive models. Readers will also be introduced to the Partition node so that they can create Training and Testing datasets.

Chapter 10, *Decision Tree Models*, introduces readers to the decision tree theory. It then provides an overview of the CHAID model so that readers become familiar with the theory, dialogs, and results of this model.

`Chapter 11`, *Model Assessment and Scoring*, speaks about assessing the results once a model has been built. This chapter discusses different ways of assessing the results of a model. Readers will also learn how to score new data and how to export these predictions.

What you need for this book

This book introduces students to the steps of data analysis. Students do not need to be experienced in analyzing data; however, an introductory statistics or data mining course would be helpful since this book's emphasis will be the point and click operations in Modeler, and neither statistical nor data mining theory. We will carefully cover theory as needed to help you understand why we are performing each of the steps in the case study, so you can safely start with this book as your very first book. However, a single case study will not provide a complete theoretical context for data mining and we will only use a single modeling algorithm in any detail.

Software demonstrations will be performed on IBM SPSS Modeler; thus, having access to Modeler is critical to enable you to follow along with step-by-step instructions. While we recognize that you might make a first pass at this content away from your computer, you should try each and every step in the book in Modeler. We have carefully narrowed the material down to the essentials. You should find that every step will serve you well when you apply what you've learned to your own data and your own situation. Since we've kept it to the basics, you should have no problem completing the entire book during the time period of a trial license of Modeler, if you do not have permanent access to Modeler. If you encounter this material in a university setting, you may be eligible for a student version.

If you don't have Modeler yet, you might want to consider watching the *Packt IBM SPSS Modeler Essentials* Video first, then installing the trial version, and then working through the book step by step. Since the two case studies are different, this will provide excellent reinforcement of the material. You will see virtually every concept twice, but with different datasets.

Who this book is for

This book is ideal for those who are new to SPSS Modeler and want to start using it as quickly as possible, without going into too much detail. An understanding of basic data mining concepts will be helpful to get the best out of the book.

Conventions

In this book, you will find a number of text styles that distinguish between different kinds of information. Here are some examples of these styles and an explanation of their meaning.

Code words in text, database table names, folder names, filenames, file extensions, pathnames, dummy URLs, user input, and Twitter handles are shown as follows: "We can include other contexts through the use of the `include` directive".

New terms and **important words** are shown in bold. Words that you see on the screen, for example, in menus or dialog boxes, appear in the text like this: "In order to download new modules, we will go to **Files** | **Settings** | **Project Name** | **Project Interpreter**."

Warnings or important notes appear like this.

Tips and tricks appear like this.

Reader feedback

Feedback from our readers is always welcome. Let us know what you think about this book-what you liked or disliked. Reader feedback is important for us as it helps us develop titles that you will really get the most out of. To send us general feedback, simply email feedback@packtpub.com, and mention the book's title in the subject of your message. If there is a topic that you have expertise in and you are interested in either writing or contributing to a book, see our author guide at www.packtpub.com/authors.

Customer support

Now that you are the proud owner of a Packt book, we have a number of things to help you to get the most from your purchase.

Downloading the example code

You can download the example code files for this book from your account at `http://www.packtpub.com`. If you purchased this book elsewhere, you can visit `http://www.packtpub.com/support` and register to have the files emailed directly to you. You can download the code files by following these steps:

1. Log in or register to our website using your email address and password.
2. Hover the mouse pointer on the **SUPPORT** tab at the top.
3. Click on **Code Downloads & Errata**.
4. Enter the name of the book in the **Search** box.
5. Select the book for which you're looking to download the code files.
6. Choose from the drop-down menu where you purchased this book from.
7. Click on **Code Download**.

Once the file is downloaded, please make sure that you unzip or extract the folder using the latest version of:

* WinRAR / 7-Zip for Windows
* Zipeg / iZip / UnRarX for Mac
* 7-Zip / PeaZip for Linux

The code bundle for the book is also hosted on GitHub at `https://github.com/PacktPublishing/IBM-SPSS-Modeler-Essentials`. We also have other code bundles from our rich catalog of books and videos available at `https://github.com/PacktPublishing/`. Check them out!

Downloading the color images of this book

We also provide you with a PDF file that has color images of the screenshots/diagrams used in this book. The color images will help you better understand the changes in the output. You can download this file from `https://www.packtpub.com/sites/default/files/downloads/IBMSPSSModelerEssentials_ColorImages.pdf`.

Errata

Although we have taken every care to ensure the accuracy of our content, mistakes do happen. If you find a mistake in one of our books-maybe a mistake in the text or the code-we would be grateful if you could report this to us. By doing so, you can save other readers from frustration and help us improve subsequent versions of this book. If you find any errata, please report them by visiting http://www.packtpub.com/submit-errata, selecting your book, clicking on the **Errata Submission Form** link, and entering the details of your errata. Once your errata are verified, your submission will be accepted and the errata will be uploaded to our website or added to any list of existing errata under the Errata section of that title. To view the previously submitted errata, go to https://www.packtpub.com/books/content/support and enter the name of the book in the search field. The required information will appear under the **Errata** section.

Piracy

Piracy of copyrighted material on the internet is an ongoing problem across all media. At Packt, we take the protection of our copyright and licenses very seriously. If you come across any illegal copies of our works in any form on the internet, please provide us with the location address or website name immediately so that we can pursue a remedy. Please contact us at copyright@packtpub.com with a link to the suspected pirated material. We appreciate your help in protecting our authors and our ability to bring you valuable content.

Questions

If you have a problem with any aspect of this book, you can contact us at questions@packtpub.com, and we will do our best to address the problem.

1

Introduction to Data Mining and Predictive Analytics

IBM SPSS Modeler is an interactive data mining workbench composed of multiple tools and technologies to support the entire data mining process. In this first chapter, readers will be introduced to the concepts of data mining, CRISP-DM, which is a recipe for doing data mining the right way, and a case study outlining the data mining process. The chapter topics are as follows:

- Introduction to data mining
- CRISP-DM overview
- The data mining process (as a case study)

Introduction to data mining

In this chapter, we will place IBM SPSS Modeler and its use in a broader context. Modeler was developed as a tool to perform data mining. Although the phrase predictive analytics is more common now, when Modeler was first developed in the 1990s, this type of analytics was almost universally called **data mining**. The use of the phrase data mining has evolved a bit since then to emphasize the exploratory aspect, especially in the context of big data and sometimes with a particular emphasis on the mining of private data that has been collected. This will not be our use of the term. Data mining can be defined in the following way:

Data mining is the search of data, accumulated during the normal course of doing business, in order to find and confirm the existence of previously unknown relationships that can produce positive and verifiable outcomes through the deployment of predictive models when applied to new data.

Several points are worth emphasizing:

- The data is not new
- The data that can solve the problem was not collected solely to perform data mining
- The data miner is not testing known relationships (neither hypotheses nor hunches) against the data
- The patterns must be verifiable
- The resulting models must be capable of something useful
- The resulting models must actually work when deployed on new data

In the late 1990s, a process was developed called the **Cross Industry Standard Process for Data Mining** (**CRISP-DM**). We will be drawing heavily from that tradition in this chapter, and CRISP-DM can be a powerful way to organize your work in Modeler. It is because of our use of this process in organizing this book's material that prompts us to use the term data mining. It is worth noting that the team that first developed Modeler, originally called Clementine, and the team that wrote CRISP-DM have some members in common.

CRISP-DM overview

The CRISP-DM is considered to be the de facto standard for conducting a data mining project. Starting with the **Business Understanding** phase and ending with the **Deployment** phase, this six-phase process has a total of 24 tasks. It is important to not get by with just focusing on the highest level of the phases, since it is well worth the effort to familiarize yourself with all of the 24 tasks. The diagram shown next illustrates the six phases of the CRISP-DM process model and the following pages will discuss each of these phases:

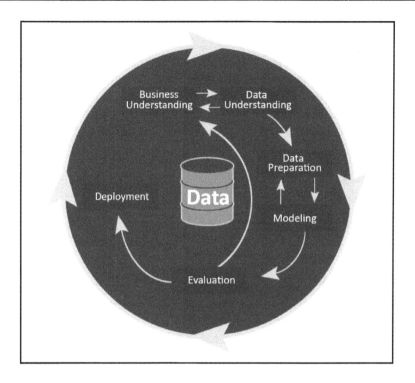

Business Understanding

The **Business Understanding** phase is focused on good problem definition and ensuring that you are solving the business's problem. You must begin from a business perspective and business knowledge, and proceed by converting this knowledge into a data mining problem definition. You will not be performing the actual **Business Understanding** in Modeler, as such, but Modeler allows you to organize supporting material such as word documents and PowerPoint presentations as part of a Modeler project file. You don't need to organize this material in a project file, but you do need to remember to do a proper job at this phase. For more detailed information on each task within a phase, refer to the CRISP-DM document itself. It is free and readily available on the internet.

The four tasks in this phase are:

- Determine business objectives
- Assess situation
- Determine data mining goals
- Produce project plan

Data Understanding

Modeler has numerous resources for exploring your data in preparation for the other phases. We will demonstrate a number of these in Chapter 3, *Importing Data into Modeler*; Chapter 4, *Data Quality and Exploration*; and Chapter 8, *Looking for Relationships Between Fields*. The **Data Understanding** phase includes activities for getting familiar with the data as well as data collection and data quality. The four **Data Understanding** tasks are:

- Collect initial data
- Describe data
- Explore data
- Verify data quality

Data Preparation

The **Data Preparation** phase covers all activities to construct the final dataset (the data that will be fed into the modeling tool(s)) from the initial raw data. **Data Preparation** is often described as the most labor-intensive phase for the data analyst. It is terribly important that **Data Preparation** is done well, and a substantial amount of this book is dedicated to it. We cover cleaning, selecting, integrating, and constructing data, in Chapter 5, *Cleaning and Selecting Data*; Chapter 6, *Combining Data Files*; and Chapter 7, *Deriving New Fields*, respectively. However, a book dedicated to the basics of data mining can really only start you on your journey when it comes to **Data Preparation**, since there are so many ways in which you can improve and prepare data. When you are ready for a more advanced treatment of this topic, there are two resources that will go into **Data Preparation** in much more depth, and both have extensive Modeler software examples: The *IBM SPSS Modeler Cookbook* (*Packt Publishing*) and *Effective Data Preparation* (*Cambridge University Press*).

The five **Data Preparation** tasks are:

- Select data
- Clean data
- Construct data
- Integrate data
- Format data

Modeling

The **Modeling** phase is probably what you expect it to be—the phase where the modeling algorithms move to the forefront. In many ways, this is the easiest phase, as the algorithms do a lot of the work if you have done an excellent job on the prior phases and you've done a good job translating the business problem into a data mining problem. Despite the fact that the algorithms are doing the heavy lifting in this phase, it is generally considered the most intimidating; it is understandable why. There are an overwhelming number of algorithms to choose from. Even in a well-curated workbench such as Modeler, there are dozens of choices. Open source options such as R have hundreds of choices. While this book is not an algorithms guide, and even though it is impossible to offer a chapter on each algorithm, `Chapter 9`, *Introduction to Modeling Options in IBM SPSS Modeler* should be very helpful in understanding, at a high level, what options are available in Modeler. Also, in `Chapter 10`, *Decision Tree Models* we go through a thorough demonstration of one modeling technique, decision trees, to orient you to modeling in Modeler.

The four tasks in this phase are:

- Select modeling technique
- Generate test design
- Build model
- Assess model

Evaluation

At this stage in the project you have built a model (or models) that appears to be of high quality, from a data analysis perspective. Before proceeding to final deployment of the model, it is important to more thoroughly evaluate the model—to be certain it properly achieves the business objectives.

Evaluation is frequently confused with model assessment—the last task of the **Modeling** phase. Assess model is all about the data analysis perspective and includes metrics such as model accuracy. The authors of CRISP-DM considered calling this phase business evaluation because it has to be conducted in the language of the business and using the metrics of the business as indicators of success. Given the nature of this book, and its emphasis on the point and click operation of Modeler, there will be virtually no opportunity to practice this phase, but in real world projects it is a critical phase.

The three tasks in this phase are:

- Evaluate results
- Review process
- Determine next steps

Deployment

Creation of the model is generally not the end of the project. Depending on the requirements, the **Deployment** phase can be as simple as generating a report or as complex as implementing a repeatable data mining process. Given the software focus of this book and the spirit of sticking to the basics, we will really only cover using models for the scoring of new data. Real world deployment is much more complex and a complex deployment can more than double the length of a project. Modeler's capabilities in this area go far beyond what we will be able to show in this book. The final chapter of this book, `Chapter 11`, *Model Assessment and Scoring*, briefly talks about some of these issues.

However, it is not unusual for the deployment team to be different than the modeling team, and the responsibility may fall to team members with more of an IT focus. The IBM software stack offers dedicated tools for complex deployment scenarios. IBM Collaboration and Deployment Services has such advanced features.

The four tasks in the **Deployment** phase are:

- Plan deployment
- Plan monitoring and maintenance
- Produce final report
- Review project

Learning more about CRISP-DM

Here are five great resources to learn more about CRISP-DM:

- The CRISP-DM document itself, found in various forms: `https://en.wikipedia.org/wiki/Cross_Industry_Standard_Process_for_Data_Mining`
- *Tom Khabaza's Nine Laws of Data Mining*: `http://khabaza.codimension.net/index_files/9laws.htm`

- The *IBM SPSS Modeler Cookbook* (*Packt Publishing*), in particular there is a more extensive introduction and an appendix with essays on the **Business Understanding** phase
- *Data Mining For Dummies*: There is no software instruction in this book, but it has an excellent chapter on CRISP-DM and also a chapter on the nine laws
- `https://www.lynda.com/SPSS-tutorials/Essential-Elements-Predictive-Analytics-Data-Mining`: This web-based course does not cover software tasks but discusses predictive analytics strategy, CRISP-DM, and the *Nine Laws of Data Mining*

The data mining process (as a case study)

As `Chapter 9`, *Introduction to Modeling Options in IBM SPSS Modeler* will illustrate, there are many different types of data mining projects. For example, you may wish to create customer segments based on products purchased or service usage, so that you can develop targeted advertising campaigns. Or you may want to determine where to better position products in your store, based on customer purchase patterns. Or you may want to predict which students will drop out of school, so that you can provide additional services before this happens.

In this book, we will be using a dataset where we are trying to predict which people have incomes above or below $50,000. We may be trying to do this because we know that people with incomes above $50,000 are much more likely to purchase our products, given that previous work found that income was the most important predictor regarding product purchase. The point is that regardless of the actual data that we are using, the principles that we will be showing apply to an infinite number of data mining problems; whether you are trying to determine which customers will purchase a product, or when you will need to replace an elevator, or how many hotels rooms will be booked on a given date, or what additional complications might occur during surgery, and so on.

As was mentioned previously, Modeler supports the entire data mining process. The figure shown next illustrates exactly how Modeler can be used to compartmentalize each aspect of the CRISP-DM process model:

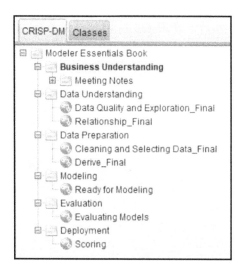

In Chapter 2, *The Basics of Using IBM SPSS Modeler*, you will become familiar with the Modeler graphic user interface. In this chapter, we will be using screenshots to illustrate how Modeler represents various data mining activities. Therefore the following figures in this chapter are just providing an overview of how different tasks will look within Modeler, so for the moment do not worry about how each image was created, since you will see exactly how to create each of these in later chapters.

First and foremost, every data mining project will need to begin with well-defined business objectives. This is crucial for determining what you are trying to accomplish or learn from a project, and how to translate this into data mining goals. Once this is done, you will need to assess the current business situation and develop a project plan that is reasonable given the data and time constraints.

Once business and data mining objectives are well defined, you will need to collect the appropriate data. Chapter 3, *Importing Data into Modeler* will focus on how to bring data into Modeler. Remember that data mining typically uses data that was collected during the normal course of doing business, therefore it is going to be crucial that the data you are using can really address the business and data mining goals:

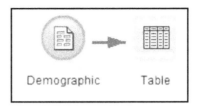

Once you have data, it is very important to describe and assess its quality. Chapter 4, *Data Quality and Exploration* will focus on how to assess data quality using the **Data Audit** node:

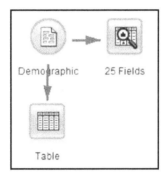

Once the **Data Understanding** phase has been completed, it is time to move on to the **Data Preparation** phase. The **Data Preparation** phase is by far the most time consuming and creative part of a data mining project. This is because, as was mentioned previously, we are using data that was collected during the normal course of doing business, therefore the data will not be clean, it will have errors, it will include information that is not relevant, it will have to be restructured into an appropriate format, and you will need to create many new variables that extract important information. Thus, due to the importance of this phase, we have devoted several chapters to addressing these issues. Chapter 5, *Cleaning and Selecting Data* will focus on how to select the appropriate cases, by using the **Select** node, and how to clean data by using the **Distinct** and **Reclassify** nodes:

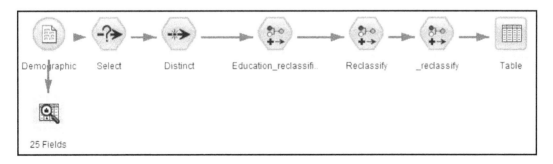

Chapter 6, *Combining Data Files* will continue to focus on the **Data Preparation** phase by using both the **Append** and **Merge** nodes to integrate various data files:

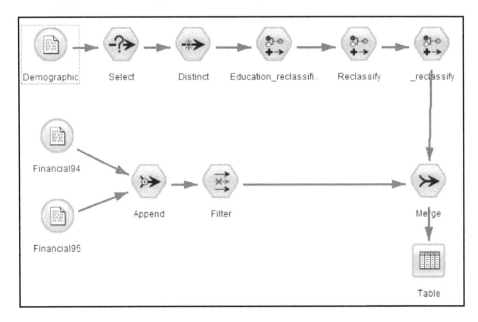

Finally, Chapter 7, *Deriving New Fields* will focus on constructing additional fields by using the **Derive** node:

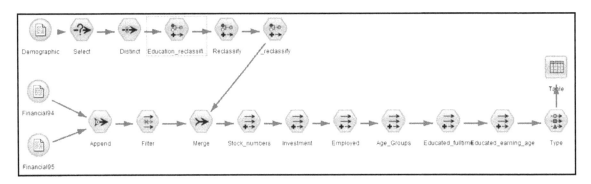

At this point we will be ready to begin exploring relationships within the data. In Chapter 8, *Looking for Relationships Between Fields* we will use the **Distribution**, **Matrix**, **Histogram**, **Means**, **Plot**, and **Statistics** nodes to uncover and understand simple relationships between variables:

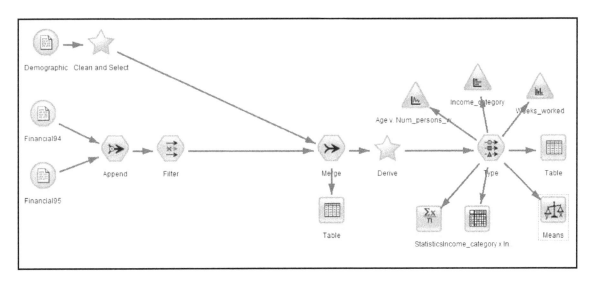

Once the **Data Preparation** phase has been completed, we will move on to the **Modeling** phase. Chapter 9, *Introduction to Modeling Options in IBM SPSS Modeler* will introduce the various types of models available in Modeler and then provide an overview of the predictive models. It will also discuss how to select a modeling technique. Chapter 10, *Decision Tree Models* will cover the theory behind decision tree models and focus specifically on how to build a CHAID model. We will also use a **Partition** node to generate a test design; this is extremely important because only through replication can we determine whether we have a verifiable pattern:

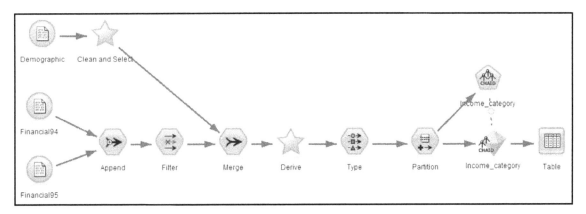

Chapter 11, *Model Assessment and Scoring* is the final chapter in this book and it will provide readers with the opportunity to assess and compare models using the **Analysis** node. The **Evaluation** node will also be introduced as a way to evaluate model results:

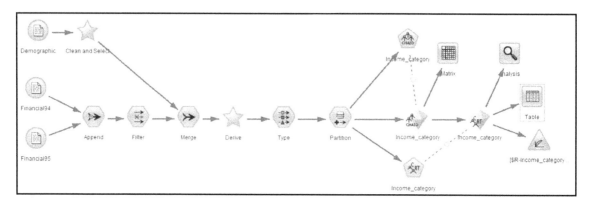

Finally, we will spend some time discussing how to score new data and export those results to another application using the **Flat File** node:

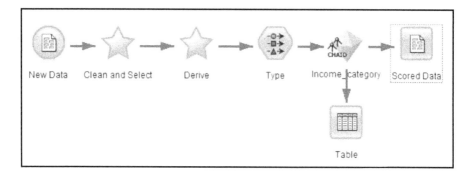

Summary

In this chapter, you were introduced to the notion of data mining and the CRISP-DM process model. You were also provided with an overview of the data mining process, along with previews of what to expect in the upcoming chapters.

In the next chapter you will learn about the different components of the Modeler graphic user interface. You also learn how to build streams. Finally, you will be introduced to various help options.

2
The Basics of Using IBM SPSS Modeler

The previous chapter introduced the notion of data mining and the CRISP-DM process model. You learned what data mining is, why you would want to use it, and some of the types of questions you could answer with data mining. The rest of this book is going to focus on how you actually do some of the aspects of data mining—reading data, exploring variables, deriving new fields, developing models, and so on. However, before we can get started with these different data mining projects, we first need to become familiar with the software that we will use to work on the data. In this chapter, you will learn the following:

- Get an overview of the Modeler interface
- Learn how to build streams
- Get an introduction to various help options

Introducing the Modeler graphic user interface

IBM SPSS Modeler can be thought of as a *data mining workbench* that combines multiple tools and technologies to support the data mining process. Modeler allows users to mine data visually on the stream canvas.

The following figure shows the different areas of the Modeler interface:

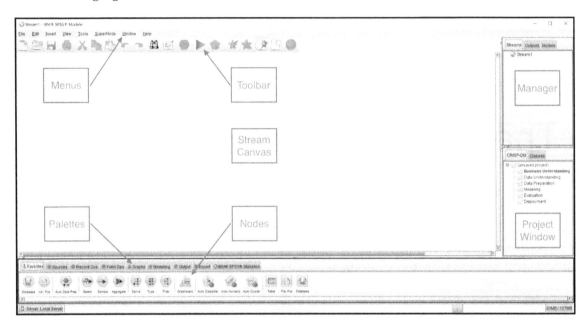

As you can see, the Modeler interface is comprised of several components, and these are described in the next few pages.

Stream canvas

The stream canvas is the main work area in Modeler. It is located in the center of the Modeler user interface. The stream canvas can be thought of as a surface on which to place icons or nodes. These nodes represent operations to be carried out on the data. Once nodes have been placed on the stream canvas, they can be linked together to form a stream.

Palettes

Nodes (operations on the data) are contained in palettes. The palettes are located at the bottom of the Modeler user interface. Each palette contains a group of related nodes that are available for you to add to the data stream. For example, the **Sources** palette contains nodes that you can use to read data into Modeler, and the **Graphs** palette contains nodes that you can use to explore your data visually. The icons that are shown depend on the active, selected palette.

The following is a brief description of each palette's functionality:

- The **Favorites** palette contains commonly used nodes. You can customize which nodes appear in this palette, as well as their order—for that matter, you can customize any palette.
- **Sources** nodes are used to access data.
- **Record Ops** nodes manipulate rows (cases).
- **Field Ops** nodes manipulate columns (variables).
- **Graphs** nodes are used for data visualization.
- **Modeling** nodes contain dozens of data mining algorithms.
- **Output** nodes present data to the screen.
- **Export** nodes write data to a data file.
- **IBM SPSS Statistics** nodes can be used in conjunction with IBM SPSS Statistics.

Modeler menus

In the upper left-hand section of the Modeler user interface, there are eight menus. The menus control a variety of options within Modeler, as follows:

- **File** allows users to create, open, and save Modeler streams and projects. Streams can also be printed from this menu.
- **Edit** allows users to perform editing operations, for example, copying/pasting objects, clearing manager tabs, and editing individual nodes.
- **Insert** allows users to insert a particular node as an alternative to dragging a node from a palette.
- **View** allows users to toggle between hiding and displaying items (for example, the toolbar or the Project window).
- **Tools** allows users to manipulate the environment in which Modeler works and provides facilities for working with scripts.
- **SuperNode** allows users to create, edit, and save a condensed stream.
- **Window** allows users to close related windows (for example, all open output windows), or switch between open windows.
- **Help** allows users to access help on a variety of topics or to view a tutorial.

Toolbar

The icons on the toolbar represent commonly used options that can also be accessed via the menus, however the toolbar allows users to enable these options via this easy-to-use, one-click alternative:

The options on the toolbar include:

- Creating a new stream
- Opening an existing stream
- Saving the current stream
- Printing the current stream
- Moving a selection to the clipboard
- Copying a selection to the clipboard
- Pasting a selection to the clipboard
- Undoing the last action
- Redoing the last action
- Searching for nodes in the current stream
- Editing the properties of the current stream
- Previewing the running of a stream
- Running the current stream
- Running a selection
- Encapsulating selected nodes into a supernode
- Zooming in on a supernode
- Showing/hiding stream markup
- Inserting a new comment
- Opening IBM SPSS Modeler Advantage

Manager tabs

In the upper right-hand corner of the Modeler user interface, there are three types of manager tabs. Each tab (**Streams**, **Outputs**, and **Models**) is used to view and manage the corresponding type of object, as follows:

- The **Streams** tab opens, renames, saves, and deletes streams created in a session.
- The **Outputs** tab stores Modeler output, such as graphs and tables. You can save output objects directly from this manager.
- The **Models** tab contains the results of the models created in Modeler. These models can be browsed directly from the **Models** tab or on the stream displayed on the canvas.

Project window

In the lower right-hand corner of the Modeler user interface, there is the project window. This window offers two ways to organize your data mining work, including:

- The **CRISP-DM** tab, which organizes streams, output, and annotations according to the phases of the CRISP-DM process model
- The **Classes** tab, which organizes your work in Modeler by the type of objects created

Building streams

As was mentioned previously, Modeler allows users to mine data visually on the stream canvas. This means that you will not be writing code for your data mining projects; instead you will be placing nodes on the stream canvas. Remember that nodes represent operations to be carried out on the data. So once nodes have been placed on the stream canvas, they need to be linked together to form a stream. A stream represents the flow of data going through a number of operations (nodes). The following diagram is an example of nodes on the canvas, as well as a stream:

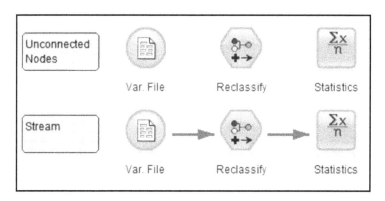

Given that you will spend a lot of time building streams, in this section you will learn the most efficient ways of manipulating nodes to create a stream.

Mouse buttons

When building streams, mouse buttons are used extensively so that nodes can be brought onto the canvas, connected, edited, and so on. When building streams within Modeler, mouse buttons are used in the following ways:

- The left button is used for selecting, placing, and positioning nodes on the stream canvas
- The right button is used for invoking context (pop-up) menus that allow for editing, connecting, renaming, deleting, and running nodes
- The middle button (optional) is used for connecting and disconnecting nodes

Adding nodes

To begin a new stream, a node from the **Sources** palette needs to be placed on the stream canvas. There are three ways to add nodes to a stream from a palette:

Method one: Click on palette and then on stream:

1. Click on the **Sources** palette.
2. Click on the **Var. File** node.

This will cause the icon to be highlighted.

3. Move the cursor over the stream canvas.
4. Click anywhere in the stream canvas.

A copy of the selected node now appears on the stream canvas. This node represents the action of reading data into Modeler from a delimited text data file. If you wish to move the node within the stream canvas, select it by clicking on the node, and while holding the left mouse button down, drag the node to a new position.

Method two: Drag and drop:

1. Now go back to the **Sources** palette.
2. Click on the **Statistics File** node and drag and drop this node onto the canvas.

The **Statistics File** node represents the action of reading data into Modeler from an IBM SPSS Statistics data file.

Method three: Double-click:

1. Go back to the **Sources** palette one more time.
2. Double click on the **Database** node.

The **Database** node represents the action of reading data into Modeler from an ODBC compliant database.

Editing nodes

Once a node has been brought onto the stream canvas, typically at this point you will want to edit the node so that you can specify which fields, cases, or files you want the node to apply to. There are two ways to edit a node.

Method one: Right-click on a node:

1. Right-click on the **Var. File** node:

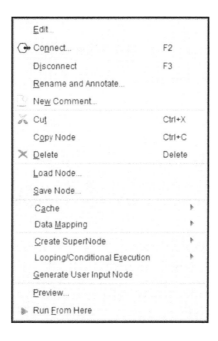

Notice that there are many things you can do within this context menu. You can edit, add comments, copy, delete a node, connect nodes, and so on. Most often you will probably either edit the node or connect nodes.

Method two: Double-click on a node:

1. Double-click on the **Var. File** node.

This bypasses the context menu we saw previously, and goes directly into the node itself so we can edit it.

Deleting nodes

There will be times when you will want to delete a node that you have on the stream canvas. There are two ways to delete a node.

Method one: Right-click on a node:

1. Right-click on the **Database File** node.
2. Select **Delete**.

The node is now deleted.

Method two: Use the *Delete* button from the keyboard:

1. Click on the **Statistics File** node.
2. Click on the *Delete* button on the keyboard.

Building a stream

When two or more nodes have been placed on the stream canvas, they need to be connected to produce a stream. This can be thought of as representing the flow of data through the nodes.

To demonstrate this, we will place a **Table** node on the stream canvas next to the **Var. File** node. The **Table** node presents data in a table format.

1. Click the **Output** palette to activate it.
2. Click on the **Table** node.

3. Place this node to the right of the **Var. File** node by clicking in the stream canvas:

At this point, we now have two nodes on the stream canvas, however, we technically do not have a stream because the nodes are not speaking to each other (that is, they are not connected).

Connecting nodes

In order for nodes to work together, they must be connected. Connecting nodes allows you to bring data into Modeler, explore the data, manipulate the data (to either clean it up or create additional fields), build a model, evaluate the model, and ultimately score the data. There are three main ways to connect nodes to form a stream that is, double-clicking, using the middle mouse button, or manually:

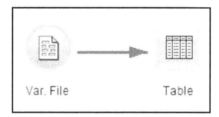

Method one: Double-click.

The simplest way to form a stream is to double-click on nodes on a palette. This method automatically connects the new node to the currently selected node on the stream canvas:

1. Select the **Var. File** node that is on the stream canvas.
2. Double-click the **Table** node from the **Output** palette.

This action automatically connects the **Table** node to the existing **Var. File** node, and a connecting arrow appears between the nodes. The head of the arrow indicates the direction of the data flow.

Method two: Manually.

To manually connect two nodes:

1. Bring a **Table** node onto the canvas.
2. Right-click on the **Var. File** node.
3. Select **Connect** from the context menu.
4. Click the **Table** node.

Method three: Middle mouse button.

To use the middle mouse button:

1. Bring a **Table** node onto the canvas.
2. Use the middle mouse button to click on the **Var. File** node.
3. While holding the middle mouse button down, drag the cursor over to the **Table** node.
4. Release the middle mouse button.

Deleting connections

When you know that you are no longer going to use a node, you can delete it. Often, though, you may not want to delete a node; instead you might want to delete a connection. Deleting a node completely gets rid of the node. Deleting a connection allows you to keep a node with all the edits you have done, but for now the unconnected node will not be part of the stream. Nodes can be disconnected in several ways:

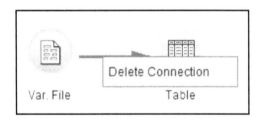

Method one: Delete the connecting arrow:

1. Right-click on the connecting arrow.
2. Click **Delete Connection**.

Method two: Right-click on a node:

1. Right-click on one of the nodes that has a connection.
2. Select **Disconnect** from the **Context** menu.

Method three: Double-clicking:

1. Double-click with the middle mouse button on a node that has a connection.

All connections to this node will be severed, but the connections to neighboring nodes will be intact.

Modeler stream rules

You may have noticed that in the previous example, we connected the **Var. File** node to the **Table** node and this worked fine. However, what if instead we tried to connect the **Table** node to the **Var. File** node? Let's try it:

1. Right-click the **Table** node.
2. Select **Connect** from the Context menu (notice that the **Connect** option does not exist).

Let's try something different:

1. Bring a **Statistics File** node onto the canvas.
2. Right-click on the **Var. File** node.
3. Select **Connect** from the **Context** menu.
4. Click the **Statistics File** node (notice that you get an error message when you try to connect these two nodes).

The reason we are experiencing these issues is that there are rules for creating Modeler streams.

Modeler streams are typically comprised of three types of nodes: **Source**, **Process**, and **Terminal** nodes. Connecting nodes in certain ways makes sense in the context of Modeler, and other connections are not allowed.

In terms of general rules, streams always start with a **Source** node (a node from the **Sources** palette), since these nodes import data. **Source** nodes can only have arrows directed out of them, but not into them. The **Var. File** node is an example of a **Source** node. This is why we can connect the **Var. File** node to a **Table** node, but we cannot connect the **Statistics file** node to the **Var. File** node. As a visual reminder, **Source** nodes are circular.

Process nodes are data preparation nodes, and they come from the **Record Ops** and **Field Ops** palettes. These nodes are hexagonal in shape and they can have arrows directed into or out of them. Technically, **Process** nodes are optional (every stream requires **Source** and **Terminal** nodes), however in reality, quite often **Process** nodes are the most commonly used nodes in a stream. For example, the **Derive** node is a process node. To see an example of how to add a process node to a stream, do the following:

1. Right-click on the **Var. File** node.
2. Select **Connect** from the **Context** menu.
3. Click the **Table** node.
4. Click the **Field Ops** palette to activate it.
5. Click on the **Derive** node.
6. Place this node in-between the **Var. File** node and the **Table** node by clicking in the stream canvas.
7. Click on the arrow connecting the **Var. File** node and the **Table** node and drag and drop the connection onto the **Derive** node, as shown in the following diagram:

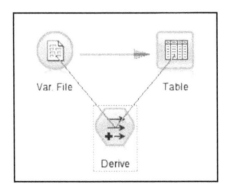

All three nodes are now connected and the **Derive** node has an arrow directed into and out of it.

Every stream always ends with a **Terminal** node. These nodes appear at the end of a stream and they can only have arrows directed into them, but not out of them. The **Table** node is an example of a **Terminal** node. This is why we can connect the **Var. File** node to a **Table** node, but we cannot connect the **Table** node to the **Var. File** node. **Terminal** nodes are found in the **Graphs** (triangle), **Modeling** (pentagon), **Output** (square), and **Export** (square) palettes.

Help options

When using Modeler, at some point we are going to need help. Modeler provides various help options.

Help menu

The most intuitive way to get help is to use the **Help** menu. As seen in the following figure, the **Help** menu provides several options:

- **Help Topics** takes you to the **Help System**, where you can search for various topics
- **CRISP-DM Help** provides an introduction to the CRISP-DM methodology
- **Application Examples** offers a variety of real-life examples of using common data mining techniques for data preparation and modeling
- **Accessibility Help** informs users about keyboard alternatives to using the mouse
- **What's This** changes the cursor into a question mark and provides information about any Modeler item you select

Dialog help

Perhaps the most useful help option is to use context sensitive help, which is available in whatever dialog box you are currently working on. For example, let's say that you are using the **Var. File** node and you either did not know how to use this node or you were unfamiliar with some of the options. First, let's open this node:

1. Right-click on the **Var. File** node.
2. Click **Edit**.
3. Now, to get help, click on the **Help** button (the icon with a question mark):

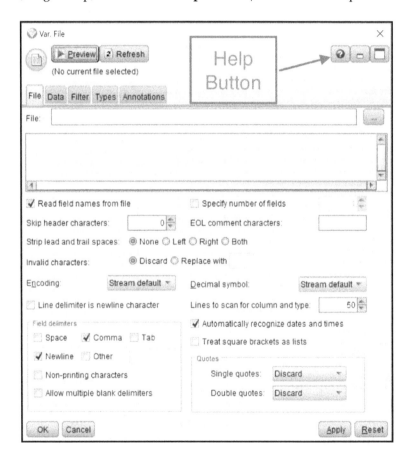

Notice that a new window explaining the different options within the **Var. File** source node appears, which provides specific information about the options in this dialog box:

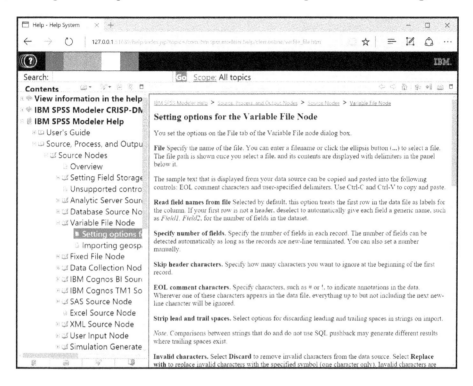

In this way, you can become familiar with this node and its options.

You can close this window and return to the stream canvas.

Summary

In this chapter, you learned about the different components of the Modeler graphic user interface. You also learned how to build streams. Finally, you were introduced to various help options.

In the next chapter, we will take a detailed look at how to bring data into Modeler. We will also discuss how to properly set up the metadata for your fields.

3
Importing Data into Modeler

The previous chapter introduced the Modeler graphic user interface. You learned where different components of the program are located, how to work with nodes and create streams, and how to use various help options. Being somewhat familiar now with the software, we are ready to get started on our data mining project. The first step is to bring data into Modeler. In this chapter, you will:

- Get an overview of the general data structure that is used in Modeler
- Learn how to read and display data in Modeler
- Get an introduction to level of measurement and field roles

Data structure

Modeler can read data from a variety of different file formats. If you take a look at the **Sources** palette, you will see that Modeler can read data from any one of the data import nodes: text files, databases, IBM SPSS Statistics or Cognos, SAS, or Excel, in addition to many others. In fact, unlike programs such as Microsoft Excel or IBM SPSS Statistics, where you can manually enter data into the program, in Modeler you must read data into the software from an external file. In this chapter, the focus will be on reading data files from free-field text files, which is a common file type. We will also briefly show you the options for reading in data from two other commonly used sources, Microsoft Excel and ODBC databases.

The following figure depicts the typical data structure used in Modeler. In general, Modeler uses a data structure in which the rows of a table represent cases and the columns of a table represent variables. In this figure, we can see that each row represents a person and each column represents a demographic characteristic of that individual. For example, in the first row we have the data for the person with the label `ID 1001`. We can see that this person is `73` years old, is a `High school` graduate, and so on:

	ID	Age	Education	Enrolled_school	Marital_status	Race	Hispanic_origin	Sex
1	1001	73	High school graduate	Not applicable	Widowed	White	All other	Female
2	1002	58	Some college but no degree	Not applicable	Divorced	White	All other	Male
3	1003	18	10th grade	High school	Never married	Asian or Pacific Islander	All other	Female
4	1004	9	Children	Not applicable	Never married	White	All other	Female
5	1005	10	Children	Not applicable	Never married	White	All other	Female
6	1006	48	Some college but no degree	Not applicable	Married-civilian spouse present	Amer Indian Aleut or Eskimo	All other	Female
7	1007	42	Bachelors degree(BA AB BS)	Not applicable	Married-civilian spouse present	White	All other	Male
8	1008	28	High school graduate	Not applicable	Never married	White	All other	Female
9	1009	47	Some college but no degree	Not applicable	Married-civilian spouse present	White	All other	Female
10	1010	34	Some college but no degree	Not applicable	Married-civilian spouse present	White	All other	Male

When data is in this format, it is very important that each row in a file has the same unit of analysis. For example, in a file where each record or row of data represents a unique employee, then the employee is the unit of analysis. In another file, each row may represent a department; in this case the department is the unit of analysis. If a project requirement is to merge these two files, you might need to aggregate the employee information so that each row represents the department.

Var. File source node

The **Var. File** source node reads data from a delimited (free-field) text file. In the following example, we will read a comma-delimited data file with field names in the first row. The file contains demographic information such as `Age`, `Education`, `Marital_status`, and so on. We will read this file into Modeler using the **Var. File** source node.

If the stream canvas is not empty, clear the stream canvas by doing the following:

1. Click the **Edit** menu, then select **Clear** stream.
2. Select the **Sources** palette.
3. Double-click on the **Var. File** node (this node should now be on the canvas).

The **Var. File** source node represents the process of reading a delimited text data file into Modeler. To link this node to a specific data file, you will need to edit the node:

1. Right-click on the **Var. File** node.
2. Click **Edit** (alternatively, double-click on the **Var. File** node).

Var. File source node File tab

The **File** tab in a source node points to the exact location of the data file you are trying to link up to the node. This tab also allows users to specify information needed to correctly bring the data into Modeler. The first thing to do in the **File** tab is to specify the data file's name and location:

1. Click on the file list button (**...**), marked with three dots, in the upper right-hand corner of the menu.
2. Navigate to where the data file is located and select the file `Demographic.txt`.
3. Click **Open**:

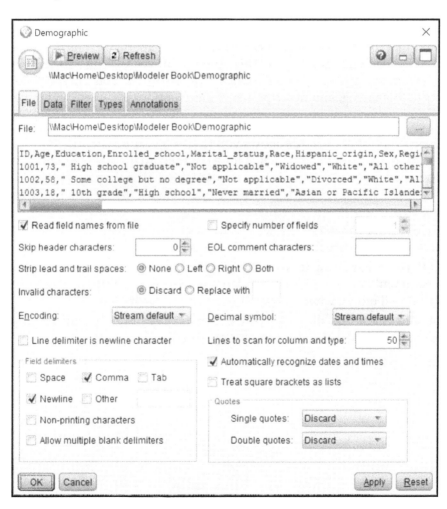

The **Var. File** dialog provides a preview of the first few lines of the data. Notice that the first line contains the field names and the data begins on the second line. This is the ideal scenario for a text file, because now Modeler can read the field names directly. Just make sure the **Read field names from file** check box is selected. By default, this option is already selected, however if the field names are not located in the first line of the file, deselect this option so that generic names, such as field 1, field 2, and so on, can be given to the fields in the dataset.

Also notice that in the preview a comma separates each field. In this example, we have a file that matches the default (**Comma**) option in the **Field delimiters** section, however this will not always be the case, so it is important that the correct delimiter(s) are selected to separate the individual fields.

Most of the default options work well in the majority of situations, however on occasion you might find that the data is not read correctly. In our experience, one of the first options to modify is **Strip lead and trail spaces**. This option removes leading and trailing blanks (extra spaces) from string fields and will often fix problems. As you can see, there are many other options in this dialog, and descriptions of these options are presented in the following list:

- **Specify number of fields** allows you to specify how many fields are in each record in the data file if all fields for a data record are not contained on a single line. If all fields for a data record are contained on a single line, then the number of fields is left unspecified and Modeler automatically calculates the number of fields.
- **Skip header characters** allows you to specify how many characters are to be read and ignored before the first record begins.
- **EOL comment characters** specifies one or more characters that denote the start of a comment or annotation. When Modeler comes across these characters in the file, it will ignore what follows until a new line is started.
- **Invalid characters** allows users to either remove or replace any character not recognized in the encoding of your operating system.

- **Encoding** refers to the text encoding method used to represent the text.
- **Decimal symbol** allows users to set either a comma or a period by using the drop-down menu.
- **Lines to scan for column and type** scans 50 rows of data (by default) to determine a field's measurement level. The measurement level is a very important concept in Modeler and this will be discussed in more detail later on in this chapter.
- **Treat square brackets as lists** treats data included between opening and closing square brackets as a single value, even if the content includes delimiter characters such as commas and double quotes.
- Single and double quotes are dealt with using drop-down menus and can either be discarded (**Discard**), matched in pairs and then discarded (**Pair & Discard**), or included as text within the field (**Include as text**).

To view the additional functionality, let's click on the **Data** tab.

Var. File source node Data tab

The **Data** tab controls the way each field is stored in Modeler, which in turn has implications for how a field can be used. Generally, the measurement level determined by Modeler is appropriate, however if you need to change this for a field, check the field's **Override** box, then click in its **Storage** cell and select the appropriate storage option.

In this example, we do not need to change anything on this tab. In our own experience, often you might need to specify the appropriate format for date and time fields here:

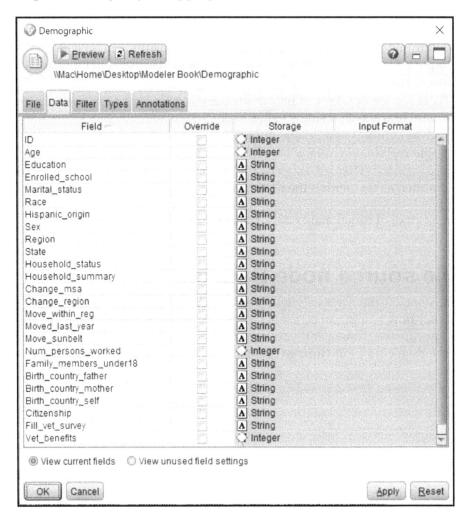

 As an aside, the **Data** tab of most source nodes functions more like the **File** tab of the **Var. File** node. Thus, this design of the **Data** tab in the **Var. File** source node makes it very easy to change the format of fields that you would otherwise need to change using a **Filler** node.

Let's click on the **Filter** tab to see the additional options.

Var. File source node Filter tab

The **Filter** tab allows users to remove and rename fields. The left **Field** column contains the field names as read from the data file. The **Field** column on the right contains the field names as they will leave this node, therefore this is where you can rename fields. The middle column shows an arrow that can be interpreted as *becomes*, and clicking on this arrow prevents fields from appearing downstream:

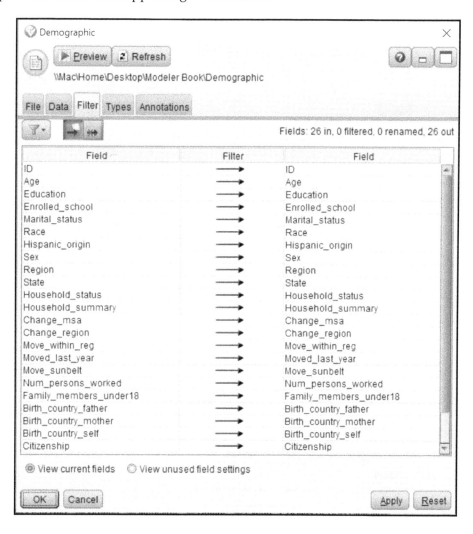

As an example, let's make a couple of changes:

1. Double-click on ID in the right **Field** column.
2. Change ID to ID_Number.
3. Click once on the arrow in the Age row:

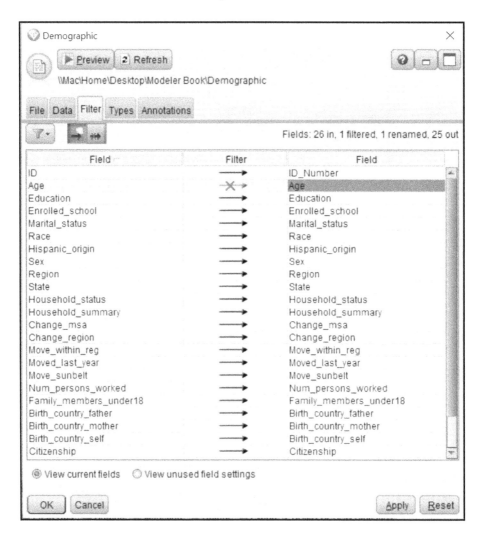

The field ID is renamed to ID_Number. The red cross on the arrow for the field Age indicates that data for the field Age will not be read downstream from this node. In fact, in the upper right-hand corner of the **Filter** tab, you can keep track of any changes that have been made. Here we can see that there are 26 fields in the original file; one of these fields has been filtered, one field has been renamed, and 25 fields will be shown downstream from this node.

Within the **Filter** tab, you can change the order of the fields (just click on the **Field** column header), exclude all fields at once, or include all fields at once. Furthermore, the **Filter** menu gives you access to numerous filter options such as including/excluding all fields, toggling between fields, removing or renaming duplicate field names, and truncating field names.

As an example, we will undo the previous changes:

1. Click the filter options button and select **Include All Fields**.
2. Click the filter options button and select **Use Input Field Names**.

The window should be the same as it was prior to changing the field ID into ID_Number and excluding the Age.

Let's briefly take a look at the **Types** tab.

Var. File source node Types tab

The **Types** tab is the most important tab within any source node. It allows users to specify field metadata and properties, and will ultimately determine how each field is used within Modeler. Because the **Types** tab is so important, we will come back to the options for the **Types** tab in the level of measurement and roles section of this chapter.

Finally, let's look at the options on the **Annotations** tab.

Var. File source node Annotations tab

The **Annotations** tab allows users to create custom names for nodes and add notes or keywords. Specifying appropriate names or tooltip texts can be especially useful when trying to distinguish several of the same kinds of nodes on the canvas, or when using a script:

Viewing data

It is important to always take a look at your data to make sure it is read correctly. The **Table** node displays the data in tabular form, with one row per record, and field names heading the columns. Let's take a look at our data:

1. Click on the **Output** palette.
2. Double-click on the **Table** node so that it is connected to the **Var. File** source node (which now has the name `Demographic`, since source nodes change their names to whatever a data file is called).

Now we need to run the table so that you can see the actual data:

1. Right-click on the **Table** node.
2. Select **Run** from the context menu.

The title bar of the **Table** displays the number of fields and records read into the table. Notice that we have 26 fields and 199,526 records:

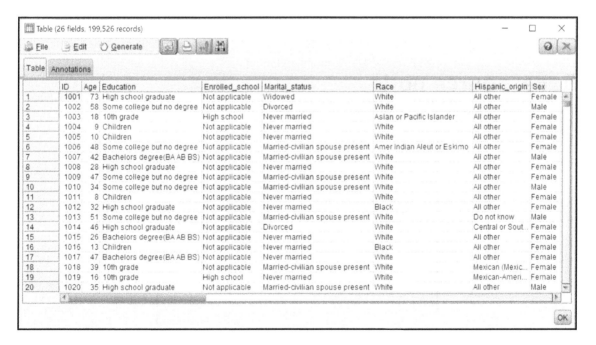

Take some time to look over the data.

The **File** menu in the **Table** window allows you to save, print, export, or publish the table. The **Edit** menu allows you to copy values or fields. The **Generate** menu allows you to automatically generate **Select** (data selection) or **Derive** (field calculation) nodes.

Now that we have done a brief check of the data file, we will close the window and return to the stream canvas, click **OK**.

Although we have closed the table, the table is still available in the **Outputs** tab. This means that we do not have to rerun the table again to see the data, which can be a big time saver if you have large data files.

To activate the outputs manager, click the **Outputs** tab:

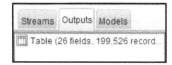

The table is still available from the manager. In fact, each output produced (table or chart) will automatically be added as a separate item in the **Outputs** tab and is available for later use or to save. To view any output, all you need to do is double-click on it.

Excel source node

The **Excel** source node allows Modeler to read data directly from Microsoft Excel:

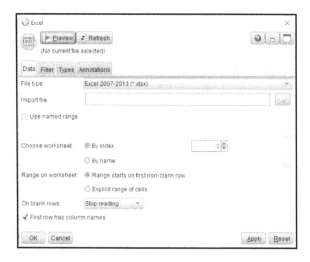

When using the **Excel** source node, you will first need to specify the type of Excel file that you are importing in the **File type** section. The filename and directory can be specified using the **Import file** list button. There are many other options in this dialog (descriptions of these options are presented in the following list). In our experience, the **On blank rows** option can be tricky because the default option specifies that once an empty row is encountered, Modeler will stop reading in data. This can be problematic because we have seen some datasets where there are blank rows (again, when a blank row is encountered, the data after the blank row is not read), or datasets where field names are in the first row. This is followed by a blank row, and then on the third row the data begins (in this case, we would only be reading in the field names).

Modeler only allows you to bring in one worksheet at a time (obviously, you can bring in other worksheets using additional **Excel** source nodes and then combine the files). The **Use named range**, **Choose worksheet**, and **Range on worksheet** options allow you to control this:

- **Use named range** specifies a named range of cells as defined in the Excel worksheet.
- **Choose worksheet** lets you specify which worksheet you want to import. Individual worksheets can be referred to either by name or index number. Index numbering begins with zero for the first worksheet, one for the second worksheet, and so forth.
- **Range on worksheet** lets you import an explicit range of cells in situations when you do not want to import the whole spreadsheet. With this option, you can either import the data beginning with the first non-blank row or specify an explicit range of cells.
- **First row has column names** indicates that the first row contains the names you want to use as field names. If not selected, field names will be generated automatically.

The **Filter**, **Types**, and **Annotations** tabs are the same in all source nodes, so we will not review these here.

Database source node

The **Database** source node imports data from a variety of packages that use **ODBC** (**Open Database Connectivity**), including Microsoft SQL Server, DB2, Oracle, and others. This node allows Modeler to read data directly from databases. Please note that before the **Database** node can be used, you must define your database as a data source (please refer to **Database** source node, under **Help Topics**, or click on dialog **Help** within a **Database** source node for additional information regarding defining data sources):

The **Mode** option (**Table** or **SQL Query**) allows you to select whether or not to view the tables/views within the database, or to enter/load an SQL query against the database.

To access data, you will need to either specify a data source or add a new database connection. Then you will need to specify which table you would like to add. Note that you can only bring in one table at a time. However, you can use another **Database** node to bring in additional tables, and these can be merged downstream.

Once you have specified the **Data source** and the **Table name**, the other options are:

- **Quote table and column names** encloses table and column names in quotation marks when queries are sent to the database.
- **Strip lead and trail spaces** controls how spaces in string fields are handled. Strings can be left and/or right trimmed.

Levels of measurement and roles

As was mentioned previously, the **Types** tab is the most important tab within any source node. Let's take a closer look at the **Types** tab:

1. Edit the **Var. File** node.
2. Click on the **Types** tab.

The **Field** column displays each field's name. The **Measurement** column determines how Modeler will use each field. Initially, fields with numeric values are typed as `Continuous`, and fields with string values are typed as `Categorical`. It is important to make sure that when you are initially reading in data, you only have fields with the measurement levels `Continuous` or `Categorical`, if this is not the case, you can manually change this.

The current display is based on 50 lines of data and thus presents partially instantiated measurement levels. Measurement levels are fully instantiated when all data passes through the node.

Instantiation refers to the process of reading or specifying information, such as the measurement level and values for a field:

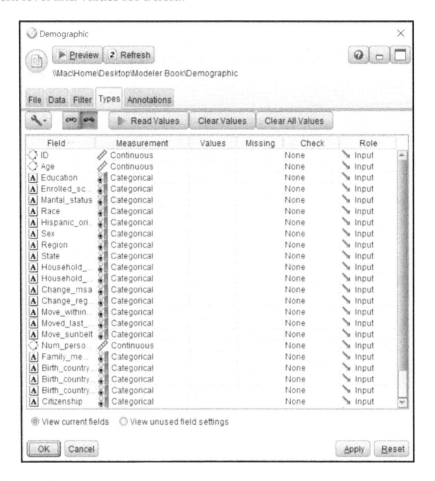

To instantiate the data:

1. Click **Read Values**.
2. Click **OK**.

Once the measurement levels have been instantiated, the values of the fields in the **Values** column of the **Types** tab are static at that point in the stream. This means that any upstream data changes will not affect the stored values of a particular field, even if you rerun the stream. To change or update the values based on new data or added manipulations, you need to edit them in the **Types** tab:

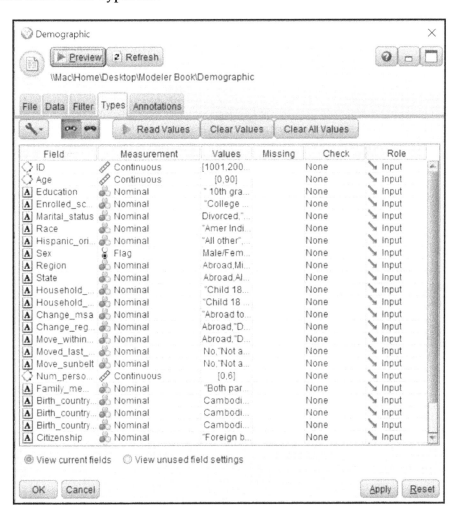

Notice that for Continuous fields, the **Values** column displays the minimum and maximum values. Also notice that the Categorical measurement level has disappeared (since it is temporary) and that string fields have now been assigned either a Flag, Nominal, or Ordinal measurement level. Also, for string fields, within the Values column the actual values are displayed.

The following table displays the definitions for each measurement level:

Measurement level	Definition
Continuous	Numeric values where the numbers have real meaning (for example, age = 42). A continuous value may be an integer, a real number, or a date/time.
Categorical	String values when the exact number of distinct values is unknown (before data is instantiated).
Flag	Data with two distinct values such as Yes/No or 1/0.
Nominal	Data with multiple distinct values, each treated as a member of a set, such as Single, Married, or Divorced.
Ordinal	Data with multiple distinct values that have an inherent order, such as 1 = Very Satisfied, 2 = Satisfied, and 3 = Neutral.
Typeless	Data that does not conform to any of the other measurement levels, or a categorical field with too many distinct values.

Measurement level is important because it determines the type of descriptive statistics and analyses appropriate for a variable. For example, for categorical (Flag, Nominal, or Ordinal) variables, counts and percentages, as well as the mode (the category with the largest number of cases), are appropriate descriptive statistics. For continuous variables, counts and percentages are less interesting as there are usually a large number of distinct values. Rather, statistics that help us understand the overall distribution of the variable are most useful. Common descriptive information for continuous variables are the minimum and maximum values and the range of the distribution. Additional summary statistics such as the mean, median, and standard deviation help us further understand the distribution.

In Modeler, the measurement level takes on greater importance because many functions, nodes, and algorithms are specially designed only for certain levels of measurement, and so certain fields cannot be used if they are not of the appropriate measurement level. Thus, it is very important to check how each variable is defined within the **Types** tab. Let's change the measurement level for the field ID. This field contains a unique reference number and is better defined as Typeless as opposed to Continuous. Also, even though the fields Vet_benefits and Year use numeric values, these fields are really categorical fields, so therefore we should change them:

1. Click in the **Measurement** cell for the field ID.
2. Choose Typeless from the list.

3. Click in the **Measurement cell** for the field `Vet_benefits`.
4. Choose `Categorical` from the list.
5. Click in the **Measurement** cell for the field `Year`.
6. Choose `Categorical` from the list.
7. Click **Read Values**.
8. Click **OK**:

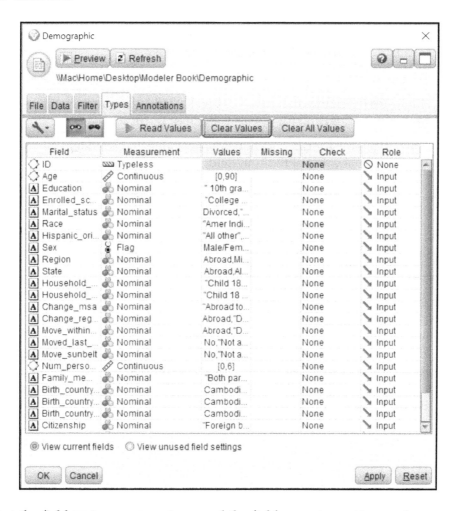

Notice that the field `ID` is now `Typeless` and the fields `Vet_benefits` and `Year` are defined as `Nominal` and `Flag`, respectively. As you will see, having the correct level of measurement is of the upmost importance.

We will discuss the **Missing** and the **Check** columns in an upcoming lesson. The **Role** column of a field specifies how each field will be used in modeling nodes. The following table displays the definition for each role:

Role	Definition
Input	The field will be an independent variable or predictor in a model.
Target	The field will be the dependent variable or an outcome for a model.
Both	The field can be used as an Input or a Target in a model. This option is only available for Association models.
None	The field will not be used in a model.
Partition	Indicates the field will be used to break up the data into separate samples for training, testing, and (optional) validation purposes.
Split	Only available for categorical fields. Specifies that a model will be built for each possible value of the split field.
Frequency	Only available for numeric fields. This role enables the field value to be used as a frequency weighting factor for the record. This option is only applicable to Linear, C&R Tree, CHAID, and Quest models.
Record ID	Only relevant for the linear node, where the specified field will be used as the unique record identifier.

You may have noticed that the role of the field ID changed from Input to None when its measurement level was changed to Typeless. This is because Typeless fields are not used in models, however they are kept so they can be used as identifiers in other nodes, such as the merge or distinct nodes. So, as with the measurement level, in Modeler field roles have implications regarding how they can be used for different functions, nodes, and algorithms. Typically, the Input role is the most common role. In our case, all of our current fields will be used as predictors in the model we will build, so Input is the appropriate role for now.

Summary

In this chapter, you learned about the general data structure that is used in Modeler. You also learned how to read and display data in Modeler. Finally, you were introduced to the measurement level and field roles concepts.

In the next chapter, we will take a detailed look at how to assess data quality in Modeler. We will also discuss how to become familiar with the fields in a dataset so that we can identify errors or unusual values.

4

Data Quality and Exploration

The previous chapter introduced the general data structure that is used in Modeler. You learned how to read and display data, and you were introduced to the concepts of the measurement level and the field roles. Now that you know how to bring data into Modeler, the next step is to assess the quality of the data. In this chapter you will:

- Get an overview of the Data Audit node options
- Go over the results of the Data Audit node
- Be introduced to missing data
- Discuss ways to address missing data

Once your data is in Modeler, you are ready to start exploring and become familiar with the characteristics of the data. You should review the distribution of each field so that you can become familiar with a dataset, but also so that you can identify potential problems that may arise. For continuous fields, you will want to inspect the range of values. For categorical fields, you will want to take a look at the number of distinct values. You will also have to consider whether you have outliers, and/or missing values (both the type and the amount).

Datasets always contain problems or errors, such as missing information and/or unusual values. Therefore, before modeling can begin, the quality of the data must be assessed. Modeler provides several nodes that can be used to investigate the integrity of the data. In our experience, the most important of these nodes is the Data Audit node. Typically, in most data mining projects, after bringing in data and making sure that it is read correctly, the Data Audit node is the next node that is used to better understand the data.

Note that in this chapter you will become familiar with the options available in the Data Audit node and the results produced by this node. However, in this chapter we are just interested in exploring the data. In the following chapter, we will fix some of the problems that we encounter.

Data Audit node options

When data is first read into Modeler, it is important to check the data to make sure it was read correctly. Typically, using a Table node can help you get a sense of the data and inform you of some potential issues that you may have. However, the Data Audit node is a better alternative to using a Table node, as it provides a more thorough look at the data.

Before modeling takes place, it is important to see how records are distributed within the fields in the dataset. Knowing this information can identify values that, on the surface, appear to be valid, but when compared to the rest of the data are either out of range or inappropriate. Let's begin by opening a stream that has the modifications we made in the previous chapter:

1. Open the `Data Quality and Exploration` stream.

This simple stream contains the `Demographic` data file that has been linked to the Var. File source, along with the modifications we previously made in the **Types** tab. In order for this stream to function correctly, you will need to ensure that the link to the data file is pointing to the correct location.

2. To use the **Data Audit** node, click on the **Output** palette.
3. Double-click on the **Data Audit** node so that it is connected to the **Var. File** node.

The **Data Audit** node provides a first look at the data by providing summary statistics, histograms, or distribution charts for each field, as well as information on missing data, outliers, and extreme scores:

1. Edit the **Data Audit** node:

The **Settings** tab controls which fields will be included in the analysis and which statistics and graphs will be reported. In our experience, most of the time the default options are ideal; however, these can certainly be modified:

- The **Default** option includes all fields in the analysis that do not have their role set to **None**.
- The **Use custom fields** option allows you to choose which fields will be included. If custom fields are selected, the **Overlay** field list allows the distribution of a categorical field to appear over the distribution of the fields selected in the **Field** list.
- The **Display** option controls whether graphs are created and which summary statistics will be calculated. Since median and mode statistics require more computational resources than basic statistics, they constitute a separate option. The **Advanced statistics** option, which we will not use in this example, displays the sum, range, variance, and kurtosis for each field.

Lets look at some additional options:

1. Click on the **Quality** tab:

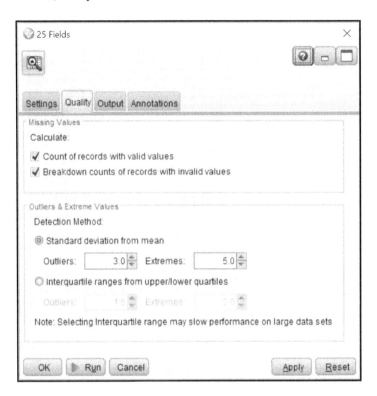

The **Quality** tab controls the options for checking missing data and determining what values are considered to be outliers and extreme cases. Again, in our experience, the default options tend to do a good job most of the time. The following is a description of the options on this tab:

- The **Count of records with valid values** option displays the total number of records with valid values for each selected field.
- The **Breakdown counts of records with invalid values** option displays the number of records with each type of invalid value for each field.
- The **Detection Method** option allows users to specify how outliers and extreme values will be determined. This can be based on either the distance away from the mean (standard deviation) or the distance away from the interquartile range.

2. To see the results of the **Data Audit** node, click the **Run** button.

Data Audit node results

Each row of the **Audit** tab of the **Data Audit** output represents a field, and the columns contain graphs, measurement level information, and summary statistics. The **Data Audit** node reports different statistics and graphs depending on the measurement level of the fields. This is one of the reasons why it is important to set the correct measurement level before running the **Data Audit** node:

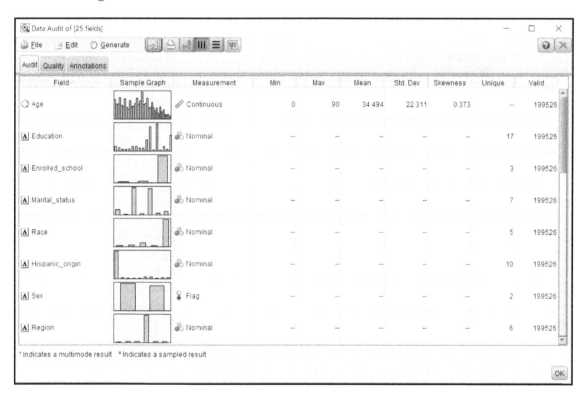

For Categorical fields, the **Data Audit** node reports the number of unique values, which is the number of unique categories. For Continuous fields, the **Data Audit** node reports on the Min (minimum), Max (maximum), Mean, standard deviation (Std. Dev, indicating the spread in the distribution), and Skewness (a measure of the asymmetry of a distribution). The Valid column reports the number of valid cases (that is, cases without missing data) for any type of field.

The **Data Audit** node produces a histogram for Continuous fields, and a bar chart for Categorical fields. Graphs are displayed as thumbnails in the initial report, but if you double-click on the thumbnails you can generate full-sized graphs.

You will want to review the distribution of each field as well as the number of valid cases. When you have a Categorical field, it is important to see how many unique values there are, and make sure there are not more than the expected number of categories. It is also important to determine how the records are distributed among the categories of a field. You might want to look for categories with either very few or a large amount of records. In either instance, this can be problematic for modeling. For Continuous fields, there is usually interest in the distribution of the data values (unusual distributions, such as those that are highly skewed or bimodal) and summary statistics (for example, having a lower minimum than expected, a higher maximum than expected, a different mean than expected, or more or less variation than expected).

In our example, all the fields have a total of 199526 valid cases, and coincidentally this is how many cases are presented in the file. Because of this, it seems that we have no missing data, but we will further explore this a little later in the chapter. In terms of our actual data mining project, we are eventually going to try to predict the income (the income field is in another file that we will bring in later). Specifically, we are going to try to determine who makes more or less than $50,000 a year. One field that is typically related to income is education. The field Education has 17 unique values; we want to ask ourselves if this is what we expected. To take a closer look at a field, you can double-click on a thumbnail.

The following screenshot displays information for the field `Education`:

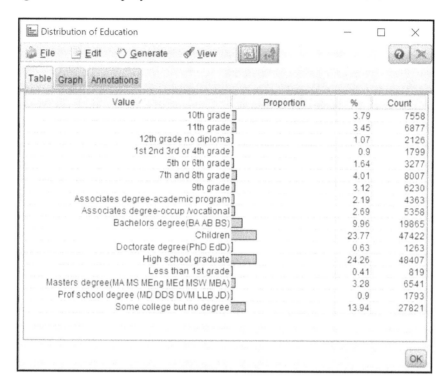

Value	Proportion	%	Count
10th grade		3.79	7558
11th grade		3.45	6877
12th grade no diploma		1.07	2126
1st 2nd 3rd or 4th grade		0.9	1799
5th or 6th grade		1.64	3277
7th and 8th grade		4.01	8007
9th grade		3.12	6230
Associates degree-academic program		2.19	4363
Associates degree-occup /vocational		2.69	5358
Bachelors degree(BA AB BS)		9.96	19865
Children		23.77	47422
Doctorate degree(PhD EdD)		0.63	1263
High school graduate		24.26	48407
Less than 1st grade		0.41	819
Masters degree(MA MS MEng MEd MSW MBA)		3.28	6541
Prof school degree (MD DDS DVM LLB JD)		0.9	1793
Some college but no degree		13.94	27821

Double-clicking on a thumbnail in the Data Audit output window creates the graph (distribution plot or histogram) in its own window. For distribution plots, category labels will appear along with count and percent summaries. This graph is added as a new object in the Outputs manager.

When we examine the distribution of the field `Education`, we can see that there are 17 different options that were used in this dataset. So, here we want to ask ourselves if the distribution of this variable makes sense. Is this what we were expecting? Do we notice any errors? Do we see any potential problems when analyzing this data? For example, often categories with very few cases (less than 5%) can be problematic for models, so we might need to exclude these values when building a model, or possibly combine them with other values, if that makes sense. Because the `Education` variable has several categories with few values, here we could begin to get an idea of how to possibly combine categories, and maybe create a new field that has the values `no high school degree`, `high school degree`, `some college`, `bachelors degree`, and `advanced degree`.

Note that the preceding example is only one way to collapse the **Education** field. Feel free to try out different options. The only caveat is that the categories should make sense (that is, do not combine the ninth grade with a doctorate degree).

One other troubling finding for this field is that we have a category called children. From an ethical perspective, maybe we should not have included children in this research. From a practical point of view, including children could artificially inflate the accurateness of our model, because it would seem that most children will probably make less than $50,000 a year.

To better see if we have children in the dataset, let's take a closer look at the field Age. The summary statistics show that the average age in the dataset is 34.5 and that the ages range from 0 to 90:

1. Double-click on the thumbnail for the field Age:

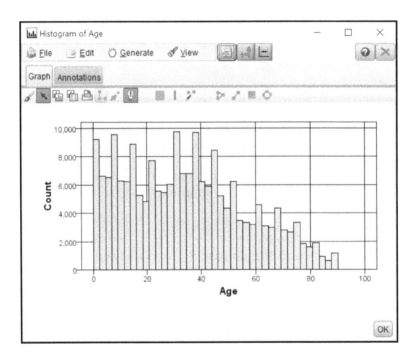

Note that there are quite a few people in this dataset that are children (their age is less than 18). We will remove these individuals in the next chapter.

2. Let's take a look at another field. Double-click on the thumbnail for the field
   `Household_summary`:

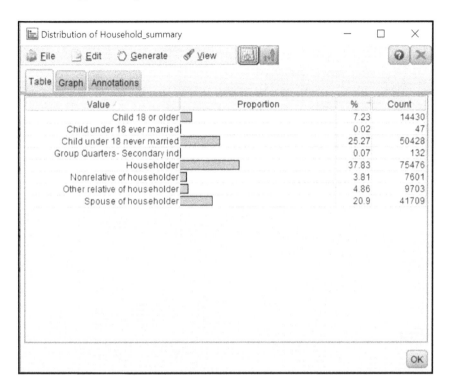

At first glance, the `Household_summary` field seems okay (aside from containing a few categories with low counts); however, upon further inspection, we can see that the category `Child under 18 ever married` is a misspelled version of the category `Child under 18 never married`. Again, we will fix this misspelling in the next chapter.

Let's take a look at another field.

3. Double-click on the thumbnail for the field `Vet_benefits`:

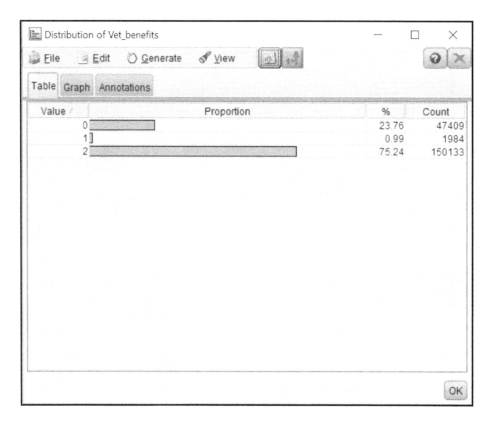

The field `Vet_benefits` is a nominal field with three values (yes, no, and not applicable); however, these values have been coded numerically. This in and of itself is not a problem (and in fact, it may be a requirement for some statistical models); however, interpretation is certainly easier when we have a label instead of a numeric value. In the next chapter, we will also show you how to fix this issue.

Let's take a look at one last field.

4. Double-click on the thumbnail for the field `Region`:

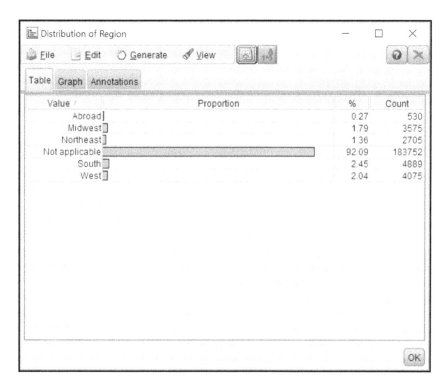

This field attempts to identify the current region where each person resides. Naturally, there are categories for different regions in the US, and there is even an `Abroad` category. However, the vast majority of respondents have selected the option `Not applicable`, and in this case, since everyone has to live either somewhere in the US or abroad, `Not applicable` really stands for missing data. Next, we will further elaborate on the notion of missing data, and after that we will discuss the options for handling missing data.

Before moving on to look at the options in the **Quality** tab of the **Data Audit** node output, take some time to further explore the other fields. For example, the birth country fields should be transformed into `Flag` fields with values of US or other values, given the low counts of most of the categories.

The Quality tab

The **Quality** tab of the **Data Audit** node output focuses on identifying outliers and missing data. It provides the number and percentages of valid values, as well as a breakdown of the different types of missing values:

1. Click on the **Quality** tab.

   Lets look at some additional information:

   - **Outliers** and **Extremes** show how many outliers and extreme values correspond to each field. Outliers and extremes only apply to `Continuous` fields, and the definitions of these values were defined in the **Quality** tab of the **Data Audit** node (by default, outliers are defined as values more than three standard deviations from the mean, and extremes are defined as values more than five standard deviations from the mean).
   - **Action** allows users to specify what action, if any, will be taken to remedy the number of outliers and extreme values.

Outlier data values, unlike other data values, can be problematic for several modeling techniques. At times, outliers can be errors in the data, for example, a schoolteacher with a salary of $1,000,000; most likely an extra zero was added during data entry. Unusual cases can be extreme scores, for example, a customer who purchased 5,000 speakers during the last month, where typically monthly orders range from 100 to 1,000 speakers per month. At other times, unusual cases can be interesting cases, for example, a patient with cystic fibrosis who is 52 years old, when the life expectancy for this disease is in the mid-30s. In addition, unusual cases can be valuable, for example, there might a small group of customers that use their cell phones a lot. This group is valuable as customers, but we might want to analyze their data separately so they do not distort the findings for typical customers. Finally, unusual cases can be a real cause for concern, for example, when investigating insurance fraud. In any of these situations, outliers can produce biased results from a model.

With regards to missing data, first of all, Modeler reports on the overall percentage of fields and records that are complete. In addition, Modeler further breaks down this information by field:

- **% Complete** expresses the percentage of the total number of complete records per field
- **Valid Records** shows the number of valid values for each field, which is followed by columns for the four types of missing values that you can have in Modeler: **Null** value, **Empty string**, **White space**, and **Blank** value
- **Impute Missing** allows users to specify if and when missing values will be imputed
- **Method** shows how missing values will be imputed

This report can be sorted by values within any of the columns by clicking on the column header.

Missing data

Missing data is different than other topics in that you cannot just choose to ignore it. This is because failing to make a choice just means you are using the default option for a procedure, which most of the time is not optimal. In fact, it is important to remember that every model deals with missing data in a certain way, and some modeling techniques handle missing data better than others.

As was alluded to previously, in Modeler there are four types of missing data:

Type of missing data	Definition
$Null$ value	Applies only to numeric fields. This is a cell that is empty or has an illegal value.
White space	Applies only to string fields. This is a cell that is empty or has spaces.
Empty string	Applies only to string fields. This is a cell that is empty. Empty string is a subset of white space.
Blank value	This is predefined code, and it applies to any type of field.

The first step in dealing with missing data is to assess the type and amount of missing data for each field. Consider whether there is a pattern as to why data might be missing. This can help determine if missing values could have affected responses. Only then can we decide how to handle it.

There are two problems associated with missing data, and these affect the quantity and quality of the data:

- Missing data reduces sample size (quantity)
- Responders may be different from nonresponders (quality—there could be biased results)

Ways to address missing data

There are three ways to address missing data:

- Remove fields
- Remove cases
- Impute missing values

It can be necessary at times to remove fields with a large proportion of missing values. The easiest way to remove fields is to use a Filter node (discussed later in the book), however you can also use the Data Audit node to do this.

 Note that in some cases missing data can be predictive of behavior, so it is important to assess the importance of a variable before removing a field.

In some situations, it may be necessary to remove cases instead of fields. For example, you may be developing a predictive model to predict customers' purchasing behavior and you simply do not have enough information concerning new customers. The easiest way to remove cases would be to use a Select node (discussed in the next chapter); however, you can also use the Data Audit node to do this.

Imputing missing values implies replacing values for fields. However, some people do not estimate values for categorical fields because it does not seem right. In general, it is easier to estimate missing values for numeric fields, such as age, where often analysts will use the mean, median, or mode.

 Note that it is not a good idea to estimate missing data if you are missing a large percentage of information for that field, because estimates will not be accurate. Typically, we try not to impute more than 5% of values.

To close out of the Data Audit node:

1. Click **OK** to return to the stream canvas.

Defining missing values in the Type node

When working with missing data, the first thing you need to do is define the missing data so that Modeler knows there is missing data, otherwise Modeler will think that the missing data is another value for a field (which, in some situations, it is, as in our dataset, but quite often this is not the case).

Although the Data Audit node provides a report of missing values, blank values need to be defined within a Type node (or **Type** tab of a source node) in order for these to be identified by the Data Audit node. The **Type** tab (or node) is the only place where users can define missing values (**Missing** column).

 Note that in the Type node, blank values and $null$ values are not shown; however, empty strings and white space are depicted by "" or " ".

To define blank values:

1. Edit the **Var.File** node.
2. Click on the **Types** tab.
3. Click on the **Missing** cell for the field Region.

4. Select **Specify** in the **Missing** column.
5. Click **Define blanks.**

Selecting **Define blanks** chooses **Null** and **White space** (remember, Empty String is a subset of **White space**, so it is also selected), and in this way these types of missing data are specified. To specify a predefined code, or a blank value, you can add each individual value to a separate cell in the **Missing values** area, or you can enter a range of numeric values if they are consecutive.

6. Type "Not applicable" in the first **Missing values** cell.
7. Hit *Enter*:

We have now specified that "Not applicable" is a code for missing data for the field **Region**.

8. Click **OK**.

In our dataset, we will only define one field as having missing data.

9. Click on the **Clear Values** button.
10. Click on the **Read Values** button:

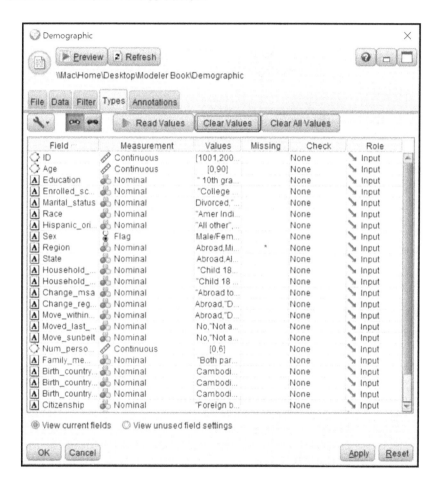

The asterisk indicates that missing values have been defined for the field Region. Now Not applicable is no longer considered a valid value for the field Region, but it will still be shown in graphs and other output. However, models will now treat the category Not applicable as a missing value.

11. Click **OK**.

Imputing missing values with the Data Audit node

As we have seen, the Data Audit node allows you to identify missing values so that you can get a sense of how much missing data you have. However, the Data Audit node also allows you to remove fields or cases that have missing data, as well as providing several options for data imputation:

1. Rerun the **Data Audit** node.

   Note that the field Region only has 15,774 valid cases now, because we have correctly identified that the Not applicable category was a predefined code for missing data.

2. Click on the **Quality** tab.

   We are not going to impute any missing values in this example because it is not necessary, but we are going to show you some of the options, since these will be useful in other situations. To impute missing values you first need to specify when you want to impute missing values. For example:

3. Click in the **Impute when** cell for the field Region.
4. Select the **Blank** & **Null Values**.

   Now you need to specify how the missing values will be imputed.

5. Click in the **Impute Method** cell for the field Region.
6. Select **Specify**.

   In this dialog box, you can specify which imputation method you want to use, and once you have chosen a method, you can then further specify details about the imputation. There are several imputation methods:

   - **Fixed** uses the same value for all cases. This fixed value can be a constant, the mode, the mean, or a midpoint of the range (the options will vary depending on the measurement level of the field).
   - **Random** uses a random (different) value based on a normal or uniform distribution. This allows for there to be variation for the field with imputed values.
   - **Expression** allows you to create your own equation to specify missing values.

- **Algorithm** uses a value predicted by a C&R Tree model.

We are not going to impute any values now so click **Cancel**.

If we had selected an imputation method, we would then:

1. Click on the field `Region` to select it.
2. Click on the **Generate** menu.

The Generate menu of the Data Audit node allows you to remove fields, remove cases, or impute missing values, explained as follows:

- **Missing Values Filter Node**: This removes fields with too much missing data, or keeps fields with missing data so that you can investigate them further
- **Missing Values Select Node**: This removes cases with missing data, or keeps cases with missing data so that you can further investigate

- **Missing Values SuperNode**: This imputes missing values:

If we were going to impute values, we would then click **Missing Values SuperNode**. This is how you can impute missing values.

Summary

This chapter focused on understanding your data. You learned about the different options available in the Data Audit node. You also learned how to look over the results of the Data Audit node to get a better feel for your data and to identify potential problems your data may have. Finally, you were introduced to the topic of missing data, and several ways to address this issue were discussed.

In the next chapter, we will begin to fix some of the problems that we found in the data. Specifically, we will use the Select node to choose the appropriate sample for our analysis. We will also use the Reclassify node to modify fields so that the distributions are appropriate for modeling. We will also use other nodes to rectify other concerns.

5

Cleaning and Selecting Data

The previous chapter focused on the data understanding phase of data mining. We spent some time exploring our data and assessing its quality. The previous chapter also mentioned that the Data Audit node is usually the first node that is used to explore and assess data. You were introduced to this node's options and learned how to look over its results. You were also introduced to the concept of missing data and shown ways to address it. In this chapter, you will learn how to:

- Select cases
- Sort cases
- Identify and remove duplicate cases
- Reclassify categorical values

Having finished the initial data understanding phase, we are ready to move onto the data preparation phase. Data preparation is the most time-consuming aspect of data mining. In fact, even in this very brief introductory book, we are devoting several chapters to this topic because it will be an integral part of every data mining project. However, every data mining project will require different types of data preparation. In the next few chapters we will introduce some very commonly used nodes. You will certainly use some of these nodes in your own work, but do not be surprised if you also have to use additional nodes that are not covered in this book.

 Data understanding is something we are always trying to achieve, because we can always learn more from and about the data. Part of data understanding is having extensive knowledge on the subject matter, part of it is exploring and assessing data quality (which we began looking at in the previous chapter), and part of it is understanding the relationships between the fields (which we will do in a later chapter).

There is no prescribed order as to how to tackle data preparation. We could certainly begin by combining various data files, or we could create new fields at this point. In our experience, a good way to start is by addressing some of the problems or errors that were found in the dataset during the initial data understanding phase. In doing this, we can get a better sense of the data. As a general point, having higher quality data will lead to more accurate predictions, which will lead to more useful and trustworthy results. For this project, based on our findings from the Data Audit node, the biggest issue with this dataset is that we have included children in the file, therefore we need to remove these cases. Let's begin by choosing the appropriate records.

Selecting cases

Often during a data mining project, you will need to select a subset of records. For example, you might want to build a model that only includes people that have certain characteristics (for example, customers who have purchased something within the last six months). The **Select** node is used when you want to select or discard a subset of records based on a specific condition. Let's go through an example of how to use the **Select** node:

1. Open the `Cleaning and Selecting data` stream.
2. Click on the **Record Ops** palette.
3. Double-click on the **Select** node so that it is connected to the **Var.File** node.
4. Right-click on the **Select** node, then click **Edit**:

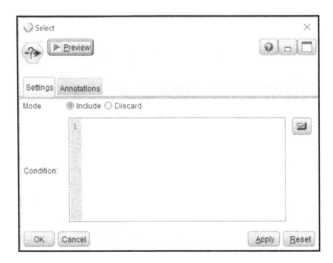

The **Select** node allows users to specify an expression either directly in the **Condition** text box or with the **Expression Builder** (the calculator icon). The **Mode** option allows you to choose whether to select (**Include**) or delete (**Discard**) records that satisfy the condition.

You can type the selection criteria into the **Condition** textbox, but it is often easier to invoke the **Expression Builder**, in which you can create an expression by clicking on the operation buttons and selecting fields and functions from list boxes.

5. Click on the **Expression Builder**.

Expression Builder

Expressions are built in the large textbox. Operations (addition, subtraction, and so on) can be pasted into the expression textbox by clicking the corresponding buttons. The **Function** list contains functions available in Modeler:

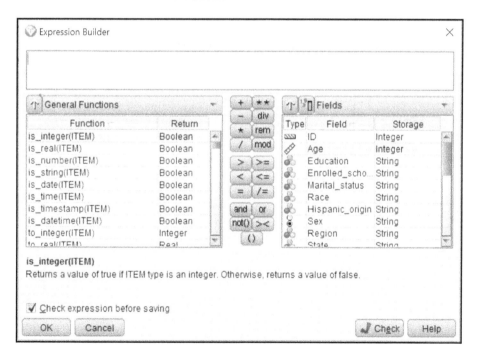

By default, a general list of functions appears, but you can use the drop-down list above the **Function** list box to display functions of a certain type (for example, date and time functions, numeric functions, logical functions, and so on). Similarly, by default, all fields (and categories within a field) in the stream are listed in the **Field** list box and can be pasted into the expression by clicking the **Insert** button after the field is selected. As an example:

1. Click on the field Education.
2. Once the field Education is selected, click on the field values button (the button with the numbers one, three, and five):

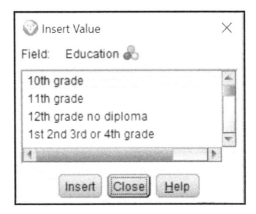

Notice that at this point we can use any of the values for the field Education if we need to. In our case, we are going to select everybody over the age of 17. To do this:

1. Close the field values dialog box.
2. Double-click on the field Age.
3. Click on the > sign.
4. Type 17.

Your selection criteria is now specifying that anyone over the age of 17 is to be selected:

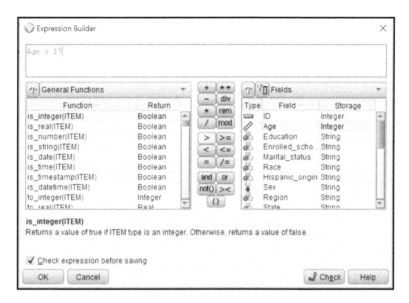

5. Click **OK**.

Because the **Mode** is set to **Include**, we are keeping anyone that meets the selection criteria and removing anyone that does not meet the criteria:

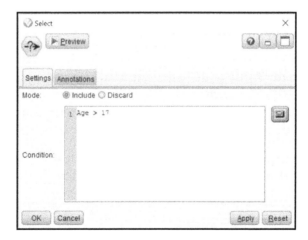

6. Click **OK**.

Now let's take a look at the results from the **Select** node:

1. Connect the **Select** node to a **Table** node.
2. Run the **Table**.

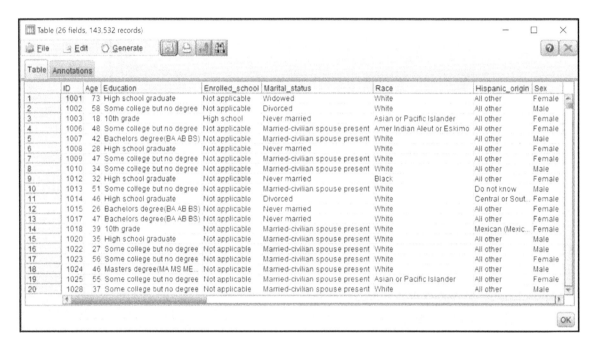

Notice that there are 143,532 records in the dataset, instead of the original 199,526 cases. At this point, all the nodes downstream of the **Select** node will analyze only records that are 18 years of age or older.

 If you run the **Table** node below the **Var. File** node, you will notice that there are 199,526 records in this table, which are all of the records in the original dataset (not shown). In this case, the selection does not apply because this table is not downstream from the **Select** node.

To quickly check on the previous command, we will rank the data file by age using a **Sort** node to ensure that we have selected all of the records of interest.

 In this example, we selected records based on one simple criterion, however we could have made the selection criteria as simple or complex as the situation required.

Sorting cases

At times it is useful to see if any values look unusual. The **Sort** node arranges cases into ascending or descending order based on the values of one or more fields. It also helps in the optimization of other nodes so that they perform more efficiently:

1. Place a **Sort** node from the **Record Ops** palette onto the canvas.
2. Connect the **Select** node to the **Sort** node.
3. Edit the **Sort** node.

You can sort data on more than one field. In addition, each field can be sorted in ascending or descending order:

1. Click on the **Field Chooser** button.
2. Select **Age** in the **Sort by:** fieldbox.
3. Click **OK**:

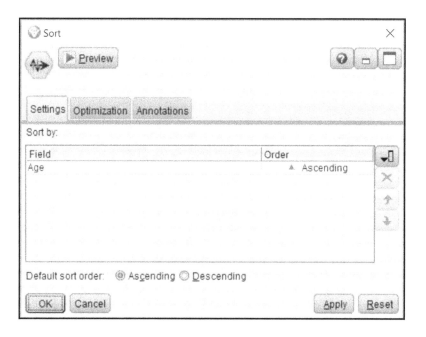

We will now rank the age cases in ascending order (the youngest people will be at the top of the file and the oldest people will be at the bottom of the file):

1. Click **OK**.

Now let's take a look at the results from the **Sort** node:

1. Connect the **Sort** node to a **Table** node.
2. Run the **Table** node:

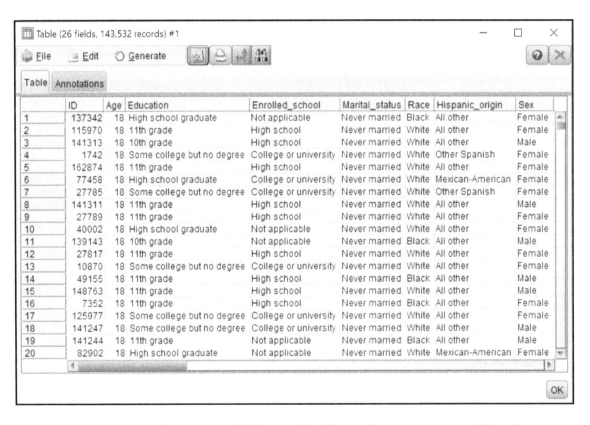

Notice that there are no longer any children in this file, as the youngest people in the dataset are 18 years old.

Identifying and removing duplicate cases

Datasets may contain duplicate records that often must be removed before data mining can begin. For example, the same individual may appear multiple times in a dataset with different addresses. The Distinct node finds or removes duplicate records in a dataset. The **Distinct** node, located in the **Record Ops** palette, checks for duplicate records and identifies the cases that appear more than once in a file so they can be reviewed and/or removed.

A duplicate case is defined by having identical data values on one or more fields that are specified. Any number or combination of fields may be used to specify a duplicate:

1. Place a **Distinct** node from the **Record Ops** palette onto the canvas.
2. Connect the **Sort** node to the Distinct node.
3. Edit the **Distinct** node.

The **Distinct** node can be a bit tricky to use; this is why we will run this node a couple of times, and hopefully in this way its options will become well-defined. The **Mode** option controls how the **Distinct** node is used. To remove duplicates in a dataset, the **Mode** should be set to **Include only the first record in each group**; in this way, the first time a record is identified it will pass, however subsequent encounters will be removed. To identify duplicates, set the mode to **Discard only the first record in each group**; this option removes the record the first time it is identified, however subsequent encounters will be kept, and in this way the duplicates will be identified. The **Create a composite record for each group** option provides a way to aggregate non-numeric fields which you can specify on the **Composite** tab to create composite records.

In this example, we will use the **Distinct** node to identify all the duplicate cases in a data file. The fields that provide the basis for identification of duplicates are selected in the **Key fields for grouping** box.

Note that the **Distinct** node will function even if the data is not sorted. However, it is best to sort the data beforehand, either by using the **Sort** node or by specifying a sort field(s) in the **Distinct** node dialog itself, in the **Within groups, sort records by: area**. Sorting makes checking the operation of the **Distinct** node more straightforward, and clearly, if there is a natural ordering to the data such that the first record in a group of duplicates is to be preferred, sorting beforehand is a necessity.

1. Place all the fields in the **Key fields for grouping:** box (by using all of the fields, we are looking for cases that are exact duplicates in all of the fields).

2. Make sure **Mode: Discard only the first record in each group** is selected:

3. Click **OK** to return to the stream canvas.
4. Connect the **Distinct** node to a **Table** node.
5. Run the **Table** node:

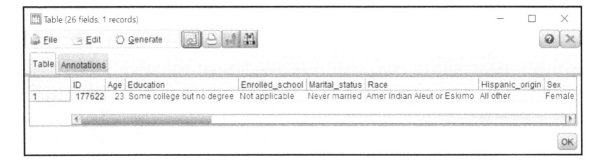

There is only one case in the data file that is an exact duplicate. We will now remove this case:

1. Edit the **Distinct** node.
2. Select **Include only the first record in each group** for the **Mode**:

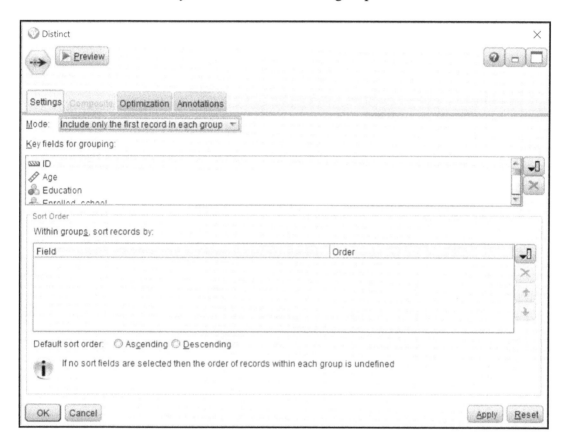

We will now remove the exact duplicate that was found previously in the data file:

1. Click **OK**.
2. Run the **Table** node.

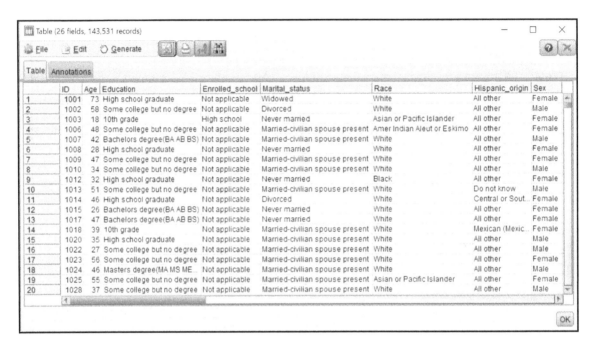

Notice that we have one fewer record in the data file since we have now removed the duplicate case.

Reclassifying categorical values

In the previous chapter, we used the Data Audit node to investigate the data file. The most critical problem that was found was that children were included in the dataset; the Select node was used to fix this issue. However, the Data Audit node also revealed additional irregularities within the data. For example, the Education field had too many categories, several of which had very low counts. In addition, the Vet_benefits field, which is a categorical variable, was coded with numeric values, so adding labels made interpretation easier.

Also, the `Household_summary` field had a misspelled version of a category that was creating an additional unnecessary category. The birth country fields needed to be transformed, given the low counts on most of the categories. We use the Reclassify node to fix all these problems.

The Reclassify node allows you to reclassify or recode the data values for categorical fields. For example, let's say that customers reported satisfaction ratings on a ten-point scale. However, after inspecting the distribution of this field, you realized that if the ratings were reclassified into a three-point (negative, neutral, or positive) scale, that would be more useful for prediction. This is exactly the function the Reclassify node performs. The reclassified values can replace the original values for a field, although a safer approach is to create a new field, thus retaining the original field as well:

1. Place a **Reclassify** node from the **Field Ops** palette onto the canvas.
2. Connect the **Distinct** node to the **Reclassify** node.
3. Edit the **Reclassify** node.

The first decision you need to make when using a **Reclassify** node is to determine what mode you want to use. The **Single** mode option is used to calculate a single new field (this is the most common use). The **Multiple** mode option is used to calculate multiple new fields where the same operations are applied to those fields. The new reclassified values will be placed into a **New field** or an **Existing field**.

Within the **Reclassify values** section:

- The **Get** button will populate the **Original value** column with values from the upstream **Type** node or **Types** tab. Alternatively, you can enter the original values directly.
- The **Copy** button will copy the values currently in the **Original value** column into the **New value** column. This is useful if you want to retain most of the original values, reclassifying only a few values.
- The **Clear new** button will clear all the values from the **New value** column (in case of errors).
- The **Auto...** button will assign a unique integer code to each value in the **Original value** column. This option is useful for replacing sensitive information (SSNs, names) with alternative identifiers, or reclassifying string values to numeric data.

Finally, you have options to use the **Original value** or a **Default value** when a value not specified in the **New value** column is encountered in the data stream. In this first example, we will reclassify the 17 values for the field Education into a new version of this variable with only five categories:

1. Click the field list button and select Education.
2. Type Education_reclassified in the **New field name** option.
3. Click the **Get** button in the **Reclassify values** section.
4. Type No high school degree in the **New value** box for the 10th grade, 11th grade, 12th grade no diploma, 1st 2nd 3rd or 4th grade, 5th or 6th grade, 7th and 8th grade, 9th grade, Children, and Less than 1st grade rows.
5. Type High school degree in the **New value** box for the High school graduate row.
6. Type Some college in the **New value** box for the Associates degree-academic program, Associates degree-occup/vocational, and Some college but no degree rows.
7. Type Bachelors degree in the **New value** box for the Bachelors degree (BA AB BS) row.
8. Type Advanced degree in the **New value** box for the Doctorate degree (PhD EdD), Masters degree (MA MS MEng Med MSW MBA), and Prof school degree (MD DDS DVM LLB JD) rows.

 Be careful not to click in the last empty row because this will create another value and cause an error when this node is run.

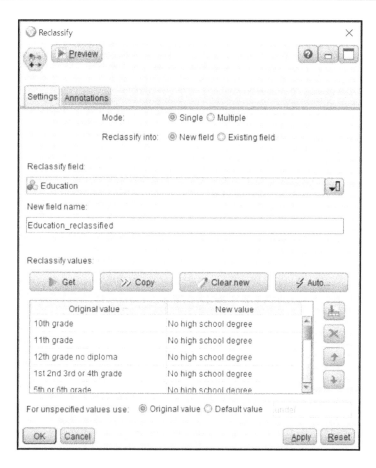

9. Click **OK**.

Now we have created a new `Education` field that has five categories instead of the 17 categories that were in the original `Education` field (to check this command, we will use the Data Audit node later in the chapter).

In this next example, we will replace the original `Vet_benefits` field with a new version that has labels instead of numeric values:

1. Place a **Reclassify** node onto the canvas.
2. Connect the `Education_reclassified` **Reclassify** node to the new **Reclassify** node.
3. Edit the new **Reclassify** node.
4. Click the field list button and select `Vet_benefits`.

5. Click **Existing field** in the **Reclassify into** option.

6. Click the **Get** button.

7. Type No in the **New value** box for the **0** row.

8. Type Yes in the **New value** box for the **1** row.

9. Type Not applicable in the **New value** box for the **2** row:

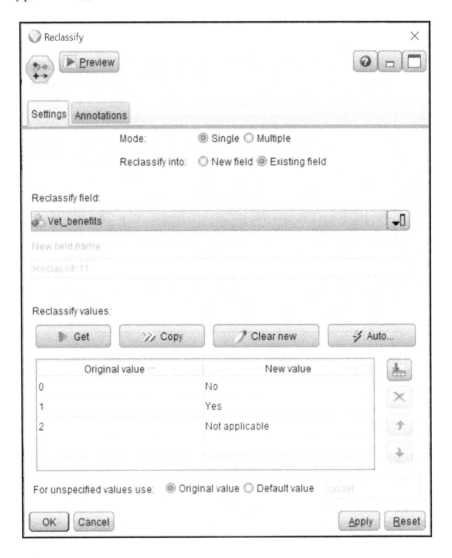

10. Click **OK**.

We have now replaced the original **Vet_benefits** field, that had numeric values, with a field that has labels that are easier to understand.

As a last example of the **Reclassify** node, we will use the **Multiple** mode option to recode the three birth country fields:

1. Place a **Reclassify** node onto the canvas.
2. Connect the `Vet_benefits` **Reclassify** node to the new **Reclassify** node.
3. Edit the new **Reclassify** node.
4. Select the **Multiple** mode.
5. Click **New field** in the **Reclassify into** option.
6. Click the field list button and select **Birth_country_father,
   Birth_country_mother**, and **Birth_country_self**.
7. In the **Field name extension** box, type `_reclassify`.
8. Click the **Get** button.
9. Type `United States` in the **New value** box for the **United-States** row.

10. Type `Other` in the **New value** box for **all the other countries** rows:

11. Click **OK**.

Now we have created three new fields that identify whether respondents or their parents were born in the US or in another country.

As a final exercise, it is a good idea to check any modifications you have made to the data. Here we will rerun the **Data Audit** node:

1. Place a **Data Audit** node onto the canvas.
2. Connect the birth country **Reclassify** node to the **Data Audit** node.
3. Run the **Data Audit** node.

   You can see that we now have 29 fields, which is more fields than we had originally. Also, the values for the field `Age` now have a range from 18 to 90, so we are excluding children from the file:

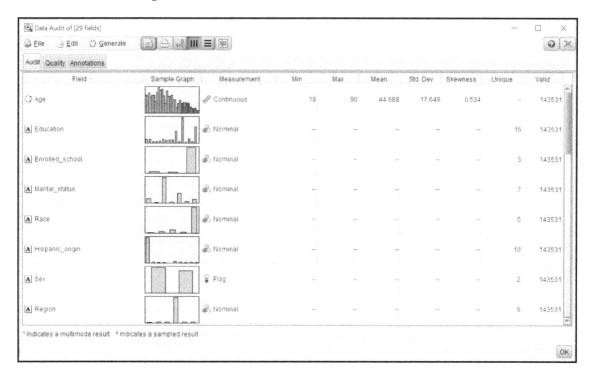

4. Double-click on the thumbnail for the field `Education_reclassified`.

The distribution of this new field with five categories is much more balanced than the original education field. Typically, this translates into making a variable a better predictor:

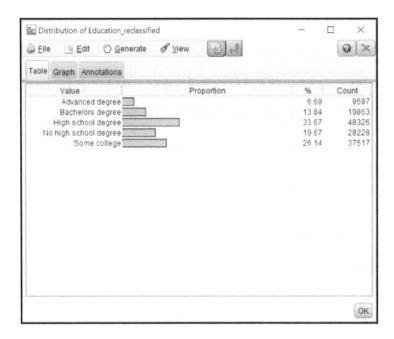

Take some time to investigate the other fields. Notice, for example, that we did not fix the misspelled version of a category for the field `Household_summary` because this is no longer a problem, since children have been excluded from the data file.

Summary

This chapter introduced the data preparation phase of data mining. The specific focus of this chapter was on fixing some of the problems that were previously identified in the data during the data understanding phase. You learned how to ensure that you are selecting the appropriate cases for analysis, and you were also exposed to the idea of sorting cases to get a better feel for the data. In addition, you learned how to identify and remove duplicate cases. Finally, you were introduced to the topic of reclassifying categorical values to address various types of issues.

In the next chapter we will expand our data preparation skills so that we can combine various data files. Specifically we will learn to combine data files using both the Merge and Append nodes.

6

Combining Data Files

The Data Preparation phase was introduced in the previous chapter, where we fixed some of the problems that were previously identified during the Data Understanding phase. You were shown how to select the appropriate cases for analysis. You were also made aware of the idea of sorting cases to get a better feel for the data. In addition, you learned how to identify and remove duplicate cases. Finally, you were introduced to the topic of reclassifying categorical values to address various types of issues. In this chapter you will:

- Learn to combine data files
- Learn how to remove unnecessary fields

As was mentioned in the previous chapter, there is no set order as to how to take on data preparation. In the previous chapter, we started preparing the data for modeling by addressing some of the problems or errors that were found in the dataset. At this point, we could have certainly continued to work on the initial data file by creating new fields, however often it is preferable to bring together all the data files that are going to be used in a project. Once this is done, there are usually more options in terms of how to creatively glean additional information from the data. This is the approach we will take in this book, but as was mentioned in the previous chapter, there is no correct sequence for preparing data. In either case, before modeling can begin, all of the different data sources must be pulled together to form a single data file. In this chapter, we introduce the methods that can be used to perform such a data manipulation.

Data mining projects will often use various data files. Sometimes these files are very similar, for example there could be files with similar customer information, but initially these files were separated by location. At other times, the files will be very different, with each containing dissimilar types of information, for example there might be demographic information in one file and financial information in another file.

We will begin this chapter by introducing the Append node as a method of joining data files that contain similar fields for separate groups of records. We will then use the Filter node to fix some problems that may occur when combining data files. Lastly, the Merge node will be introduced as a method of joining data files that contain different types of information for the same records.

Combining data files with the Append node

Similar pieces of information for different groups of records may be stored in different data files. There is often a need to collectively analyze such data, possibly to compare performance over subsequent years or to discover group differences. To analyze such information within Modeler, the data files must be combined into one single file. The Append node joins two or more data sources together so that information held for different groups of records can be analyzed and compared. The following diagram depicts how the Append node can be used to combine two separate data files that contain similar information:

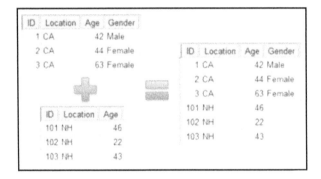

Let's go through an example of how to use the Append node to combine data files:

1. Open the **Append** stream.
2. Run a **Table** node from each source node so that you are familiar with each data file (not shown).

Notice the number of cases in each file. Also notice that one file has financial data for 1994 while the second file has financial data for 1995:

1. Place an **Append** node from the **Record Ops** palette to the right of the two source nodes.
2. Connect the source node labeled **Financial94** to the **Append** node.
3. Connect the source node labeled **Financial95** to the **Append** node.
4. Connect the **Append** node to a **Table** node:

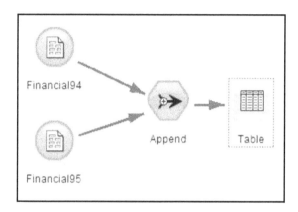

5. Edit the **Append** node.
6. Click the **Append** tab.

The Append node joins two or more data files by reading and passing all of the records from the first data source, then reading and passing the records from the second data source, and so on. The order in which the data sources are read is defined by the order in which they are attached to the Append node. The first attached data source is named the main dataset and, by default, its format is used to define the structure of the data leaving the Append node.

The Append node assumes that the data entering via the other datasets has a similar, if not identical, structure to that of the primary dataset. This node joins data by the field's **Name** in the data file, although it can also match by **Position** (this option is generally not recommended because if there happen to be any fields that are missing from a file, or if the fields have been ordered differently, this would be problematic).

The fields to be included in the newly combined data file are listed in the **Output Field** column. The **Include fields from** option gives you the ability to change the way the fields within the data files will be retained.

When there are different numbers of fields contained within the data sources (inputs) the Append node uses the following rules:

- If a data source has fewer fields than the main dataset, then the records from this data source are padded with the undefined value ($null$) for the missing fields.
- If a data source has more fields than the main dataset, then the extra fields are, by default, filtered from the stream, but there is an option that allows all the fields to be input from all datasets. If fields are input from all datasets, then the records from sources not containing these fields are padded with the undefined value ($null$).

Let's combine the two files. To do this:

1. Click the **All datasets** option:

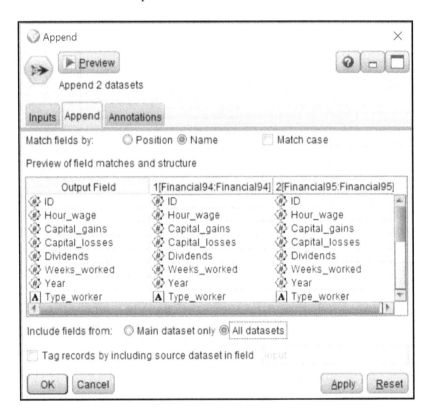

By selecting the **All datasets** option, fields found in any of the data sources will be retained in the stream. Although we will not use the **Tag records by including source dataset in field** option in this example, this option creates a field identifying from which data source a record came, which can be extremely useful if you are interested at a later point in comparing cases from different files.

2. Click the **Inputs** tab:

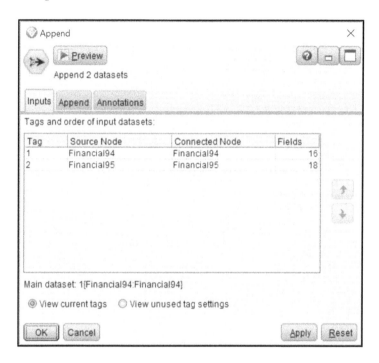

The order of the inputs, given in **Tags and order of input datasets** section, controls the order in which the records are read into the **Append** node. To promote or demote an individual input, select it and use the up or down buttons. The **Tag** column controls the name of the categories for the field, identifying them from which data source a record came from. You can also rename these values to better identify the files you are combining.

3. Click **OK**.
4. Run the **Table**.
5. Scroll to the end of the file:

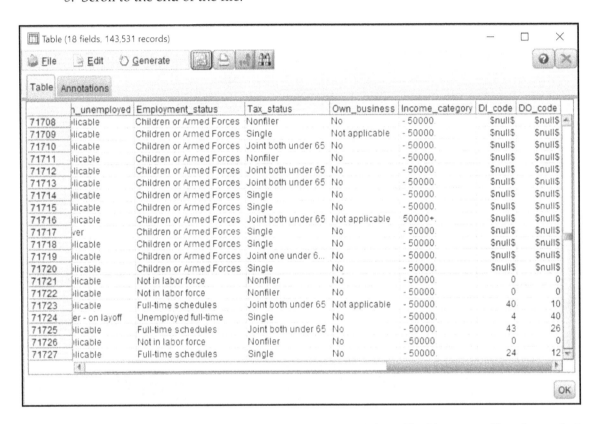

Notice that we now have 143,531 cases in the combined data file. If you scroll to the end of the file, you will notice that for the last two fields, DI_code and DO_code, the data file from 1994 is missing this information. This is because we began collecting these codes in 1995, therefore this information was unavailable for the 1994 dataset. For this reason, we now have a lot of missing data for these two fields. Since we need to use data from both of these years to build our model, we will remove these two fields because we do not want to keep fields that have such a large proportion of missing data.

 Note that in this example, and in the following example for the Merge node, only two data files were joined, however there is no limit as to how many data files can be joined at one time.

Removing fields with the Filter node

Whereas the Select node works on records, the Filter node works on fields. The Filter node discards fields, renames fields, and maps fields from one source node to another. Often, a Filter node is used to remove fields that have one of two potential problems:

- A large proportion of missing records
- All (or almost all) records having the same value

In our case, we have two fields that have a large portion of missing values, therefore we will remove these fields:

1. Place a **Filter** node from the **Field Ops** palette to the right of the **Append** node.
2. Connect the **Append** node to the **Filter** node.
3. Right-click the **Filter** node, then click **Edit**.

The **Filter** node (or **Filter** tab of a source node) allows data to pass through it and has two main functions:

- Removing unwanted fields
- Renaming fields

The left column of a **Filter** node lists the field names as the data enters the node. The right column of a **Filter** node shows the field names as the data leaves the node. By default, the lists are the same.

The text at the top of the dialog box indicates the number of fields entering the **Filter** node, the number of fields filtered, the number of fields renamed, and the number of fields leaving the node.

Previously, we showed you how to change a field name, so we will not repeat that here. To demonstrate how to remove fields from the data stream, we will filter out the fields DI_code and DO_code:

1. Click on the arrow next to the fields DI_code and DO_code:

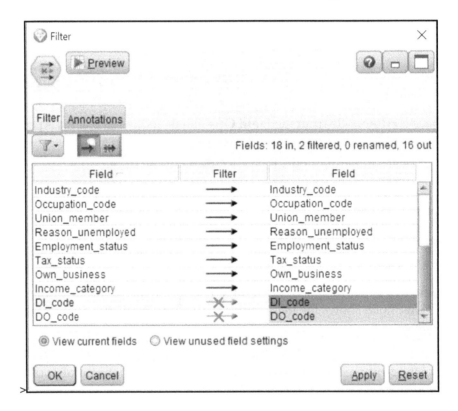

Notice that we have removed two fields, as the top of the dialog indicates that **18** fields entered the **Filter** node, but only 16 fields are leaving the **Filter** node.

2. The **Filter options** menu provides a set of options that are useful when working with a large number of fields. Click the **Filter options** button (the icon that looks like a funnel).

Filter options include removing or including all fields, toggling the remove/include settings for all fields, removing or renaming duplicate field names, anonymizing field names, and editing multiple response sets. Removing or renaming duplicate fields is especially helpful when working with database files with many fields, since it provides an easy way of setting the filter options for all fields.

3. Click **OK**.

Now let's take a look at the results from the **Filter** node:

1. Connect the **Filter** node to the **Table** node.
2. Run the stream:

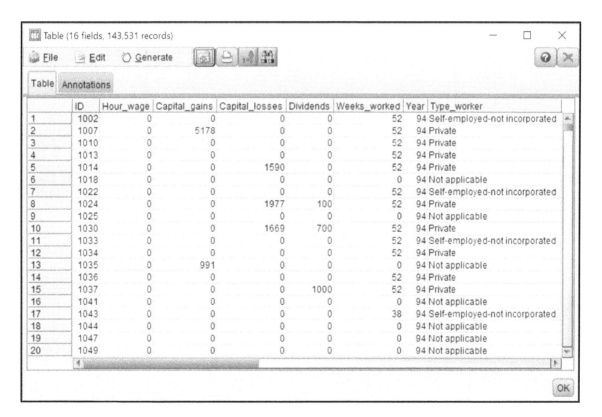

Notice that we have the same number of records as before, however the last two fields have been removed.

Combining data files with the Merge node

In many organizations, different pieces of information for the same individuals are held in separate locations. To be able to analyze such information within Modeler, the data files must be combined into one single file. The Merge node joins two or more data sources so that information held for an individual in different locations can be analyzed collectively. The following diagram shows how the Merge node can be used to combine two separate data files that contain different types of information:

Like the Append node, the **Merge** node is found in the **Record Ops** palette. This node takes multiple data sources and creates a single source containing all or some of the input fields.

Let's go through an example of how to use the Merge node to combine data files:

1. Open the **Merge** stream.

    The **Merge** stream contains the files we previously appended, as well as the main data file we were working with in earlier chapters.

2. Place a **Merge** node from the **Record Ops** palette on the canvas.
3. Connect the last **Reclassify** node to the **Merge** node.
4. Connect the **Filter** node to the **Merge** node.

 Like the **Append** node, the order in which data sources are connected to the **Merge** node impacts the order in which the sources are displayed. The fields of the first source connected to the **Merge** node will appear first, followed by the fields of the second source connected to the **Merge** node, and so on.

5. Connect the **Merge** node to a **Table** node:

6. Edit the **Merge** node

Since the **Merge** node can cope with a variety of different situations, the **Merge** tab allows you to specify the merging method.

There are four methods for merging:

- **Order**: It joins the first record in the first dataset with the first record in the second dataset, and so on. If any of the datasets run out of records, no further output records are produced. This method can be dangerous if there happens to be any cases that are missing from a file, or if files have been sorted differently.
- **Keys**: It is the most commonly used method, used when records that have the same value in the field(s) defined as the key are merged. If multiple records contain the same value on the key field, all possible merges are returned.
- **Condition**: It joins records from files that meet a specified condition.
- **Ranked condition**: It specifies whether each row pairing in the primary dataset and all secondary datasets are to be merged; use the ranking expression to sort any multiple matches from low to high order.

Let's combine these files. To do this:

1. Set **Merge Method** to **Keys**.

   Fields contained in all input sources appear in the **Possible keys** list. To identify one of more fields as the key field(s), move the selected field into the **Keys for merge** list. In our case, there are two fields that appear in both files, ID and Year.

2. Select ID in the **Possible keys** list and place it into the **Keys for merge** list:

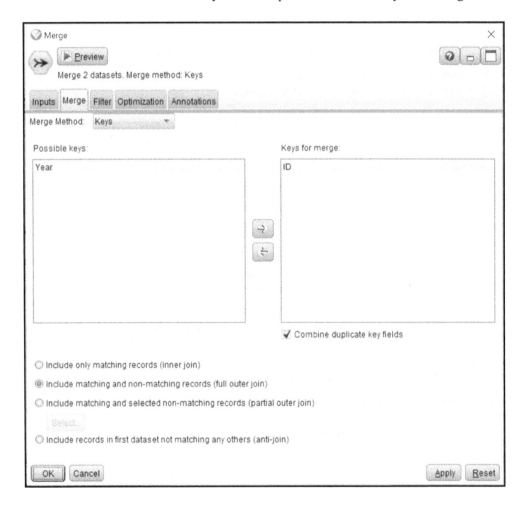

There are five major methods of merging using a key field:

- **Include only matching records (inner join)** merges only complete records, that is, records; that are available in all datasets.
- **Include matching and non-matching records (full outer join)** merges records that appear in any of the datasets; that is, the incomplete records are still retained. The undefined value ($null$) is added to the missing fields and included in the output.
- **Include matching and selected non-matching records (partial outer-join)** performs left and right outer-joins. All records from the specified file are retained, along with only those records from the other file(s) that match records in the specified file on the key field(s). The **Select...** button allows you to designate which file is to contribute incomplete records.
- **Include records in first dataset not matching any others (anti-join)** provides an easy way of identifying records in a dataset that do not have records with the same key values in any of the other datasets involved in the merge. This option only retains records from the dataset that match with no other records.
- **Combine duplicate key fields** is the final option in this dialog, and it deals with the problem of duplicate field names (one from each dataset) when key fields are used. This option ensures that there is only one output field with a given name, and this is enabled by default.

The Filter tab

The **Filter** tab lists the data sources involved in the merge, and the ordering of the sources determines the field ordering of the merged data. Here, you can rename and remove fields. Earlier, we saw that the field Year appeared in both datasets; here we can remove one version of this field (we could also rename one version of the field to keep both):

1. Click on the arrow next to the second `Year` field:

The second `Year` field will no longer appear in the combined data file.

The Optimization tab

The **Optimization** tab provides two options that allow you to merge data more efficiently when one input dataset is significantly larger than the other datasets, or when the data is already presorted by all or some of the key fields that you are using to merge:

1. Click **OK**.
2. Run the **Table**:

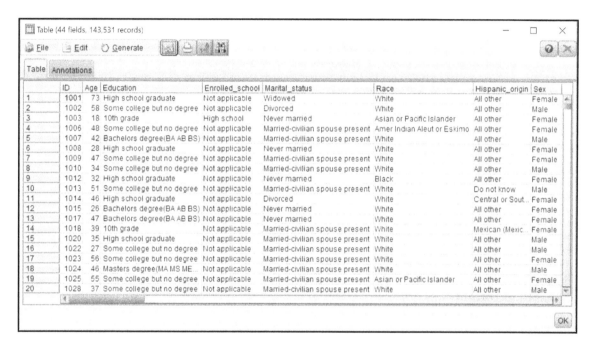

All of these files have now been combined. The resulting table should have 44 fields and 143,531 records.

In this chapter, all the combined data sources had a similar file structure in that one person defined a case. Thus the data is at the person level. Often, though, a person does not define cases. For example, purchase data is often held in a file containing one record per purchase. Although beyond the scope of this book, it is worth noting that to analyze this at the customer level, the data must be restructured so that there is one record per customer that contains summary information. The Aggregate node can create a new file so that each record contains information such as the total amount spent, average amount spent on certain goods, and total number of purchases. Alternatively, it is often useful to have data arranged so that each field represents a particular category and each record stores information whether or not a case falls into that category. The Set To Flag node may be used to transform a single field containing a set of categories into a collection of flag fields within a record to easily determine which products were purchased.

Summary

This chapter introduced the Append node as a method of joining data files that contain similar fields for separate groups of records. You also learned how to use the Filter node to remove or rename fields. Finally, you were introduced to the Merge node to join data files that contained different information for the same records.

In the next chapter, we will continue to work on our data preparation skills so that we can extract more information from the data. Specifically, we will learn to how to use the Derive node to create various types of additional fields.

7
Deriving New Fields

We have now spent several chapters on the data preparation phase of data mining. We have learned how to select and sort cases, how to identify and remove duplicate cases, how to reclassify and filter fields, and how to combine different types of data files. In this chapter you will learn how to create additional fields by:

- Deriving fields as formulas
- Deriving fields as flags
- Deriving fields as nominals
- Deriving fields as conditionals

A very important aspect of every data mining project is to extract as much information as possible. Every project will begin with some data, but it is the responsibility of the data miner to gather additional information from what is already known. In our experience, this can be the most creative and challenging aspect of a data mining project. For example, you might have survey data, but this data might need to be summed for more information, such as a total score on the survey, or the average score on the survey, and so on. In other words, it is important to create additional fields. This chapter focuses on how to create new fields based on information from other fields.

So how do we know what fields to create? The newly created fields must provide supplementary information with regards to the project goals. For our project, the goal is to develop a model that will help us predict the income category (above or below $50,000). It is therefore important to consider how each current field in the dataset might relate to this outcome. This exercise will help you determine which additional fields could be useful for both the development of the model and to further your understanding of the issue at hand. Additionally, consideration of how each field might relate to the outcome can also assist you in the removal of fields that confound the results, as often data files contain fields that either comprise part of the outcome field or occur after the outcome. As an exaggerated example, let's say we are trying to predict low birth-weight babies. We would obviously have a field that identifies the baby's birth-weight and some characteristics of the mother. We might then define a low birth-weight baby as any newborn that weighs less than 2,500 grams, thus the outcome field would have values greater than 2,500 grams and less than 2,500 grams. Because of this classification, we can no longer use the original continuous weight field to predict the weight category, since it is part of the outcome field. Additionally, if the mother suffered post-partum depression, we could not use this field as a predictor of birth weight because this occurred after the baby's birth.

Modeler has several nodes that can create additional fields, however the Derive node is the most commonly used node because it is extremely flexible. The Derive node creates new fields from one or more existing fields. Let's go through some examples of how to use the Derive node:

1. Open the stream **Derive**.
2. Place a **Derive** node from the **Field Ops** palette onto the canvas.
3. Connect the **Type** node to the new **Derive** node.
4. Right-click the new **Derive** node, then click **Edit**.

The first decision you need to make when using a Derive node is to determine what mode you want to use. The **Single** Derive mode option is used to calculate a single new field (this is the most common option). The **Multiple** Derive mode option is used to calculate multiple new fields where the same operations are applied to all of those fields. The name of the new field is entered in the **Derive field** textbox, as shown in the following screenshot:

The **Derive** node offers six different methods of creating a new field. Click on the **Derive as** drop-down list to reveal the options:

Formula	The new field is created from a CLEM expression.
Flag	The new field will have a true or false response (flag), reflecting a specified expression.
Nominal	The new field will have values assigned from members of a specified set.
State	The new field's value represents one of the two states. Switching between these states is triggered by specified conditions.
Count	The new field is based on the number of times a specified condition is true.
Conditional	The new field is the result of one of two expressions, depending on the value of a condition.

In this chapter, we will create new fields using the **Formula**, **Flag**, **Nominal**, and **Conditional** options. The **State** and **Count** options are typically used with transactional data.

Once the type of derivation is chosen, the dialog box changes accordingly. The measurement level of the field to be derived can be explicitly set using the **Field type** option.

Derive – Formula

Deriving a field as a **Formula** is extremely common, especially when working with continuous fields. Some of the most common methods of deriving a field as a formula include creating total scores, change scores and ratios. Our data file does not contain many continuous fields, however we do have several income related fields (capital gains, capital losses, and dividends) in the dataset that might be able to shed insight. Clearly, since we are predicting income, we cannot use the actual fields, capital gains, capital losses, or dividends, because all of these fields contribute to a person's overall income, and including them would create a biased model. However, rather than using actual investment dollars, we could investigate if having investments relates to income. Therefore, in order to determine if someone has investments, we first need to create a temporary field, which we will call Stock_numbers, which simply adds up capital gains, capital losses, and dividends. If someone has a value on this new field, then we will know they have investments. To create a new field:

1. Type Stock_numbers in the **Derive field** textbox.

   You can type the equation in the **Formula** textbox, but it is easier to invoke the **Expression Builder**, in which you can create an expression by clicking the functions, operations, and fields from list boxes.

2. Click the **Expression Builder** button.
3. Click on Capital_gains in the **Fields** list box, then click the insert button (the yellow arrow).

4. Click on the plus (+) button.
5. Double-click on `Capital_losses` in the **Fields** list box.
6. Click on the plus (+) button.
7. Double-click on `Dividends` in the **Fields** list box:

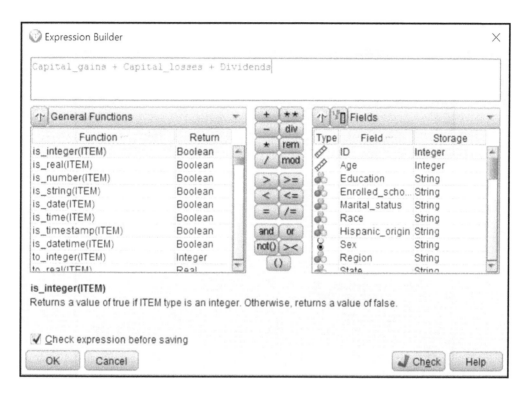

8. Click **OK**.

We can now see the formula that will be used to create the new temporary field, Stock_numbers:

9. Click **OK**.

Now that we have identified how much each person made on their investments, let's create the field we set out to create.

Derive – Flag

Deriving a field as a flag is similar to deriving a field as a formula except that the expression you create will ultimately result in one of two categorical values. One of the most common methods of deriving a field as a flag is to identify whether something of interest has occurred (for example, purchasing a product, visiting a website, and so on). In this example, we will take the Stock_numbers field and collapse it into those people who have an investment and those that do not:

1. Place a **Derive** node onto the canvas.
2. Connect the Stock_numbers node to the new **Derive** node.
3. Edit the new **Derive** node.
4. Type Investment in the **Derive field** textbox.
5. Click **Flag** on the **Derive as** drop-down list.
6. Click the **Expression Builder** button.
7. Double-click on Stock_numbers in the **Fields** list box.
8. Click the greater than (>) button.
9. Type 0.

10. Click **OK**:

This equation is saying that if someone has a value greater than zero on the field Stock_numbers, the Investment field will be assigned the value T, otherwise they will be assigned the value F.

11. Click **OK**.

As an additional example of creating a flag field, let's investigate the field Weeks_worked. Certainly, we would expect the number of weeks that someone has worked to be associated with income. One simple thing we might want to do is identify which customers have worked in the past year. For this next example, we will create a new field, Employed, which will be True if the weeks worked value is greater than zero:

1. Place a **Derive** node onto the canvas.

2. Connect the **Investment** node to the new **Derive** node.
3. Edit the new **Derive** node.
4. Type `Employed` in the **Derive field** textbox.
5. Click **Flag** on the **Derive as** drop-down list.
6. Click the **Expression Builder** button.
7. Double-click on `Weeks_worked` in the **Fields** list box.
8. Click the greater than (>) button.
9. Type `0`.
10. Click **OK**:

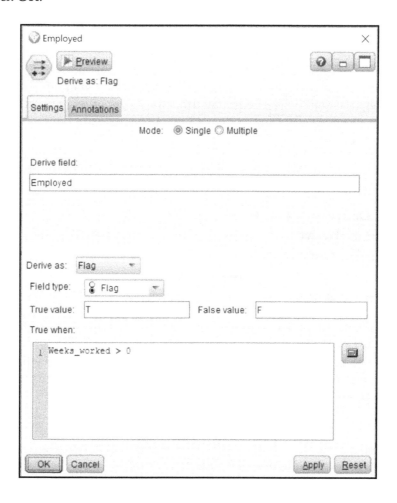

We have now created a field that identifies which customers have worked in the past year.

11. Click **OK**.

Derive – Nominal

One limitation of deriving a field as a flag is that you can only create a field with two outcomes. Deriving a field as a **Nominal** allows you to create a field with many categories. One of the most common uses of deriving a field as a **Nominal** is to transform a continuous field into a categorical field with multiple groups (for example, age groups, income groups, and so on).

 It is common in data mining to create multiple versions of a field to see if one version is a better predictor in a model. If we wanted to create categories that were of equal width, equal size, or were based on standard deviations, the Binning node could be used instead.

In this example, we will modify the Age variable by classifying Age into a categorical variable called Age_Groups, which is the Age field banded into six groups, Young, Thirties, Forties, Fifties, Sixties, and Retired:

1. Place a **Derive** node onto the canvas.
2. Connect the **Derive** node named Employed to the new **Derive** node.
3. Edit the new **Derive** node.
4. Type Age_Groups in the **Derive field** textbox.
5. Click **Nominal** on the **Derive as** drop-down list.

The dialog box contains two options to be completed for each member of the **Nominal** field. **Set field to** specifies a value in the new field when a particular condition is met. **If this condition is true** specifies the condition for a particular value. Modeler will test if the conditions are true and assign the value stored in the **Set field to** box to the first condition that applies. The **default** value is assigned if no condition applies:

1. Type Young in the first **Set field to** textbox.
2. Type Age <=29 in the **If this condition is true** textbox.
3. Type Thirties in the next **Set field to** textbox.
4. Type Age >= 30 and Age <=39 in the **If this condition is true** textbox.

5. Type `Forties` in the third **Set field to** textbox.
6. Type `Age >= 40 and Age <=49` in the **If this condition is true** textbox.
7. Type `Fifties` in the fourth **Set field to** textbox.
8. Type `Age >= 50 and Age <=59` in the **If this condition is true** textbox.
9. Type `Sixties` in the fifth **Set field to** textbox.
10. Type `Age >= 60 and Age <=69` in the **If this condition is true** textbox.
11. Type `Retired` in the sixth **Set field to** textbox.
12. Type `Age >= 70` in the **If this condition is true** textbox:

We have now created a six-category version of the `Age` field.

13. Click **OK**.

Derive – Conditional

Deriving a field as a conditional is similar to deriving a field as a flag except that, typically, the expressions tend to be more complex, as they usually involve multiple fields or specific values of a field. One of the most common methods of deriving a field as a conditional is to contrast a group of interest with others.

With regards to our data, from previous research we know that education is related to income. We also know that employment status is associated with income. We already have an education field and a field identifying the number of weeks that someone has worked. However, we do not have a field that combines these two pieces of information. In this next example, we will create a new field called `Educated_fulltime`, that will identify people that have either a bachelor's degree or an advanced degree and have worked for 52 weeks in the past year:

1. Place a **Derive** node onto the canvas.
2. Connect the **Derive** node named `Age_Groups` to the new **Derive** node.
3. Edit the new **Derive** node.
4. Type `Educated_fulltime` in the **Derive field** textbox.
5. Click **Conditional** on the **Derive as** drop-down list.
6. Type `(Education_reclassified = "Bachelors degree" or Education_reclassified = "Advanced degree") and Weeks_worked = 52` in the **If** textbox.
7. Type `'Yes'` in the **Then** textbox.
8. Type `'No'` in the **Else** textbox.

   Be sure to include the single quotes around the values in the **Then** and **Else** textboxes, as text values must be put between single quotes:

We have now created a field that identifies college graduates that work full-time.

9. Click **OK**.

The previous example combined information from education and weeks employed. We also know that age is related to income. For this last example, we will create a new field called Educated_earning_age that identifies people that have either a bachelor's degree or an advanced degree and are between the ages of 35 and 60 (the optimal earning age):

1. Place a **Derive** node onto the canvas.
2. Connect the **Derive** node named Educated_fulltime to the new **Derive** node.
3. Edit the new **Derive** node.

4. Type `Educated_earning_age` in the **Derive field** textbox.

5. Click **Conditional** on the **Derive as** drop-down list.

6. Type `(Education_reclassified = "Bachelors degree" or Education_reclassified = "Advanced degree") and (Age >= 35 and Age <=60)` in the **If** textbox.

7. Type `'Yes'` in the **Then** textbox.

8. Type `'No'` in the **Else** textbox:

We have now created a field that identifies college graduates that are of the optimal earning age. We could certainly create additional fields, but these examples show the general idea of how to create additional fields.

9. Click **OK**.

Once you have completed all of your data preparation, there are still a couple of things that need to be done before you can begin to build your models. First of all, you need to make sure that all of your data is instantiated (fully read). This is crucial because all fields need to be instantiated before any model can use them. Instantiation is accomplished by adding a Type node to the end of your stream:

1. Place a **Type** node onto the canvas.
2. Connect the **Derive** node named `Educated_earning_age` to the **Type** node.
3. Edit the **Type** node.
4. Click the **Read Values** button.

The data has now been read, so a model can now use the new fields. It is also useful at this point to specify, within the **Type** node, the different roles each field will play in the models. Most fields will typically be an **Input** (predictor), but there will be exceptions. Make the following changes to the data:

1. Make sure that the following fields have their roles set to `None`, as they will not be used in our current model: `ID`, `Year`, `Hour_wage`, `Capital_gains`, `Capital_losses`, `Dividends`, and `Stock_numbers`.
2. Given that the goal of our project is to predict the categorical field, `Income_category`, this field should have its role set to `Target`:

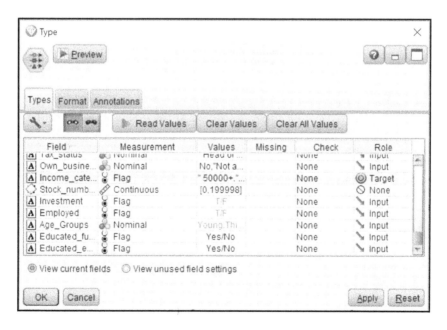

3. Click **OK**.

We can now take a look at the variables we created:

1. Connect the **Type** node to the **Table** node.
2. Run the **Table**.
3. Scroll to the end of the file:

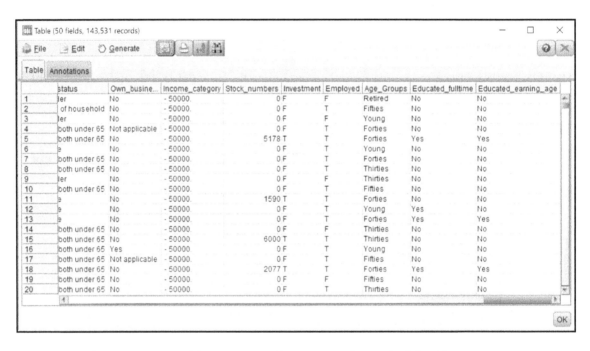

	status	Own_busine...	Income_category	Stock_numbers	Investment	Employed	Age_Groups	Educated_fulltime	Educated_earning_age
1	ler	No	- 50000.	0 F		F	Retired	No	No
2	of household	No	- 50000.	0 F		T	Fifties	No	No
3	ler	No	- 50000.	0 F		F	Young	No	No
4	both under 65	Not applicable	- 50000.	0 F		T	Forties	No	No
5	both under 65	No	- 50000.	5178 T		T	Forties	Yes	Yes
6	e	No	- 50000.	0 F		T	Young	No	No
7	both under 65	No	- 50000.	0 F		T	Forties	No	No
8	both under 65	No	- 50000.	0 F		T	Thirties	No	No
9	ler	No	- 50000.	0 F		F	Thirties	No	No
10	both under 65	No	- 50000.	0 F		T	Fifties	No	No
11	e	No	- 50000.	1590 T		T	Forties	No	No
12	e	No	- 50000.	0 F		T	Young	Yes	No
13	e	No	- 50000.	0 F		T	Forties	Yes	Yes
14	both under 65	No	- 50000.	0 F		F	Thirties	No	No
15	both under 65	No	- 50000.	6000 T		T	Thirties	No	No
16	both under 65	Yes	- 50000.	0 F		T	Young	No	No
17	both under 65	Not applicable	- 50000.	0 F		T	Fifties	No	No
18	both under 65	No	- 50000.	2077 T		T	Forties	Yes	Yes
19	both under 65	No	- 50000.	0 F		F	Fifties	No	No
20	both under 65	No	- 50000.	0 F		T	Thirties	No	No

Notice that the six new variables we created appear at the end of the file.

When deriving new fields, the type of missing data and the type of new field created interact to affect how missing data is handled. When a numeric field is created with a formula, if any of the fields in the formula have a null value ($null$), the answer returned will be a null value ($null$). On the other hand, if a **Nominal**, **Conditional**, or **Flag** field is created, a missing value on a field that is used in a **Flag**, **Nominal**, or **Conditional** derivation will not prevent Modeler from using the remaining fields to calculate a value for the new field. Thus, you need to keep this behavior in mind when creating new fields.

Summary

This chapter introduced the Derive node. The Derive node can perform many different types of calculations so that users can extract more information from the data. These additional fields can then provide insight that may not have been apparent. In this chapter you learned that the Derive node can create fields as formulas, flags, nominals, or conditionals.

In the next chapter, we will continue to explore our data by discovering simple relationships between outcome fields and predictor fields. Specifically, readers will learn to use several statistical and graphing nodes to determine which fields are related to an outcome variable.

8
Looking for Relationships Between Fields

The previous chapters have focused on data preparation. You learned how to select and sort cases, how to identify and remove duplicate cases, how to reclassify and filter fields, how to combine different types of data files, and how to derive additional fields. Now that the dataset has been prepared, in this chapter you will learn how to assess the following:

- Relationships between categorical variables
- Relationships between categorical and continuous variables
- Relationships between continuous variables

One major aspect of a data mining project is the development of a model; however, investigating simple relationships among variables can be extremely important in answering questions about what motivated a project. You may find, for example, that certain customer behaviors are associated with weather events, or purchasing specific products is associated with certain demographic characteristics. Although these patterns are not substitutes for a full model, they can often be used along with a model.

In Modeler, the techniques used to examine the relationships between fields depend on the measurement level of the fields in question. This is true for both exploring relationships in either tabular or graphical format. In fact, Modeler restricts the fields that appear in specific dialogs to those fields that meet a particular measurement level. Hence, it is extremely important to set the level of measurement correctly.

Researchers explore data to search for interesting relationships between fields. Typically, the relationship between the target field and the predictors is investigated. You will want to see which fields are strongly associated with the target and which fields are not; one reason to do so is to reduce the number of fields as inputs for a modeling node, but another reason, as was previously stated, is to investigate specific research questions.

Note that in this chapter, only relationships between two fields, say X and Y, are investigated. If no relationship is found, you cannot immediately conclude that X is not relevant for predicting Y in a model with additional predictors. Why is this the case? Let's suppose, for example, that the relationship between gender and income appears to be nonexistent. Does this finding imply that gender should not be used for predicting income? The answer to this question is a bit more complicated than you might expect, because there can be interaction effects between predictors. While gender itself may not be a good predictor, the effect of another predictor may be different depending on whether a person is male or female. In that case, leaving gender out of a model may reduce the model's accuracy.

The opposite may be true as well. Suppose there is a statistically significant relationship between gender and income. At this point in the data mining process, business understanding becomes important. Even though the difference in income between the two groups might seem large enough to the analyst, a business user of this data or of the final model should be consulted to ascertain whether this difference is indeed substantively or practically large enough. It is important to remember that the best models are not developed in isolation by the analyst, but instead are developed with continuing interaction with those who understand the data, and that the business questions are addressed from both a practical and operational perspective.

In this chapter, we will use several nodes from the **Graphs** and **Output** palettes to start exploring relationships between fields.

Relationships between categorical fields

The most common technique for describing categorical data is to create a **summary table** or **graph** indicating the number and percentage of cases falling into each category of a variable. In this section, we will discuss two nodes, the Distribution and Matrix nodes, that allow us to investigate the distribution of and relationships between categorical variables.

Distribution node

The Distribution node allows you to visually assess the distribution of a categorical field so that you can see the frequency and percentage of each category. This node also allows you to see the relationship between two categorical fields. Let's go through an example of how to use the Distribution node:

1. Open the Relationship stream.
2. Place a **Distribution** node from the **Graphs** palette onto the canvas.
3. Connect the **Type** node to the **Distribution** node.
4. Edit the **Distribution** node.

To see the distribution of a categorical field, place a field in the **Field** drop-down list:

1. Click the **Field** drop-down arrow.
2. Select the field Income_category:

3. Click **Run**. You will get the following output on screen:

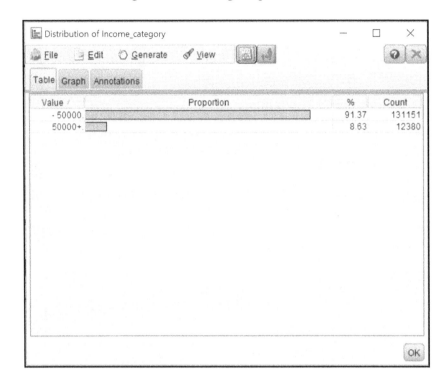

You can see that about 91% of people fall into the less than $50,000 group. This information is important to know because the field Income_category will be the target in our model. Whenever the distribution of any field is unbalanced (with many more people falling into one group rather than another), this can be problematic for a model, especially when this is the distribution of the outcome field. We will have more to say about unbalanced samples a little later in the book.

The Distribution node not only allowed us to explore the distribution of a categorical variable, but it also allows us to visually assess the relationship between two categorical fields, in this case Income_category and Investment. To do this:

1. Edit the **Distribution** node.
2. Click the **Color** drop-down arrow.
3. Select the field Investment.

4. Click **Normalize by color**:

The **Normalize by color** option scales the bars of the bar chart so that they take up the full width of the graph—this overlays values equal to a proportion of each bar, making comparisons across categories much easier, as seen in the following screenshot.

5. Click **Run**:

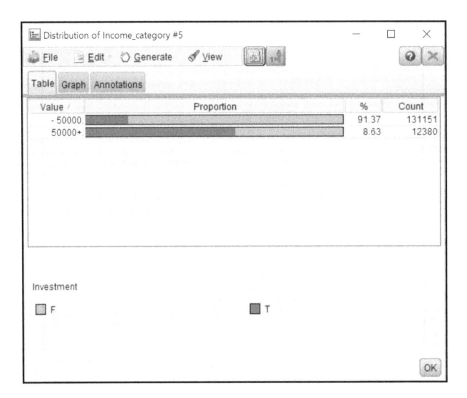

We can now see the relationship between the fields `Income_category` and `Investment`. If there was no relationship between the fields, the proportions of the bars would be the same for each group. Not surprisingly, this is not the case, as it seems that people who have investments are more likely to have incomes greater than $50,000 then people who have incomes less than $50,000.

This graph allows us to visually inspect how these fields are related to each other. However, in order to quantify this relationship, we can use the Matrix node.

Matrix node

The Matrix node creates a cross tabulation table that shows the relationships between fields. It is most commonly used to show the relationship between two categorical fields, but it can also show the relationships between flag fields or numeric fields. The Matrix node shows us how values of one field are related to those of a second field.

In this example, we will use the Matrix node to see whether there is a statistically significant relationship between the fields `Income_category` and `Investment`, that is, we are going to quantify what we previously observed with the Distribution node. To do this:

1. Place a **Matrix** node on the canvas.
2. Connect the **Type** node to the **Matrix** node.
3. Edit the **Matrix** node.

   The default setting of the **Fields** option (**Selected**) will display the fields selected in the **Rows** and **Columns** boxes (one field in each). This will create the cross tabulation that we want between two categorical fields.

   Note that only one field for **Rows** and one field for **Columns** can be selected. Thus, the Matrix node will produce only one matrix at a time.

4. Click the **Fields** list button in the **Rows** list and select `Income_category`.
5. Click the **Fields** list button in the **Columns** list and select `Investment`:

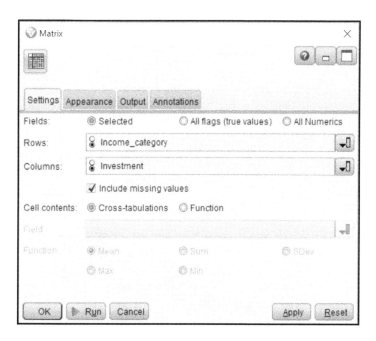

Now we will be able to determine if people with investments are more likely to fall into one income category or another.

If you were to run the node right now, the default table would contain counts in the cells of the matrix and the results of a Chi-square test of independence. Counts are definitely useful, but similar to when we ran the Distribution node, requesting percentages can really assist with interpretation (the **Normalize by color** option provided percentages). Different percentages, expected values, and residuals can be requested by using the **Appearance** tab. We will ask for column percentages in order to compare the impact of having investments with respect to income:

Although you can ask for any type of percentage, traditionally researchers request percentages based on the predictor field in order to better understand the effects of said fields on the target field.

1. Click the **Appearance** tab.
2. Select **Percentage of column**.
3. Click the **Run** button. You will get the following output:

Income_category		F	T
- 50000.	Count	109319	21832
	Column %	95.493	75.148
50000+.	Count	5160	7220
	Column %	4.507	24.852

Cells contain: cross-tabulation of fields (including missing values)

Chi-square = 12,168.98, df = 1, probability = 0

Examining the matrix table, there appears to be a difference in the distribution between having and not having investments across the income categories. For instance, only 4.5% of the people that fall into the less than $50,000 group have investments, whereas 24.9% of the people that fall into the more than $50,000 group have investments. This is a big difference between these groups. These percentages represent what we previously observed within the Distribution node. Furthermore, the Chi-square test probability value of zero further confirms the conclusion that investments are related to income category.

Recall from your statistics courses that results are statistically significant whenever a probability value is less than .05.

At this point in the data mining process, business understanding becomes pertinent. The difference in percentages between the two groups certainly seems large enough to be important, but business users of this data or of the final model should be consulted to determine whether this difference is indeed substantively or practically large enough. As mentioned earlier, the analyst does not develop the best models in isolation, but instead by continually interacting with those who understand the data and the business questions being addressed from a practical and operational perspective.

Relationships between categorical and continuous fields

When working with categorical variables, frequency tables and graphs containing counts and percentages are appropriate summaries. For continuous variables, because there are typically so many unique values, that counts and percentages can quickly become less useful and unwieldy, so traditionally we turn to the mean as the summary statistic of choice, since it provides a single measure of central tendency. In this section, we will discuss two nodes, the Histogram and Means nodes, that allow you to investigate the distribution and relationships of continuous and categorical variables.

Histogram node

The Histogram node shows the distribution of values for continuous fields. To use the Histogram node:

1. Place a **Histogram** node on the canvas.
2. Connect the **Type** node to the **Histogram** node.
3. Edit the **Histogram** node.

To see the distribution of a continuous field, place a field in the **Field** drop-down list:

1. Click the **Field** drop-down arrow.
2. Select the field Num_persons_worked, as shown in the following screenshot:

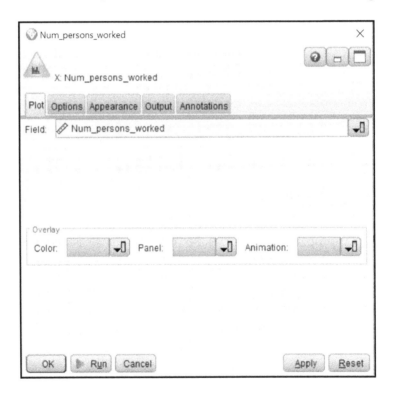

3. Click **Run** and you will get the following output:

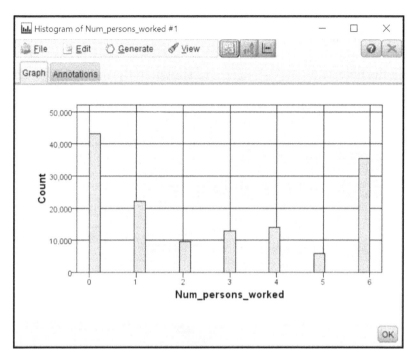

We are now seeing the distribution of the number of people that work. In an ideal world, it would be nice for continuous fields to have normal distributions (a bell-shaped curve). Here, you can easily see that the distribution of this field is not normal, as most values are on either end of the distribution. Is this problematic? Well, it depends on the type of model that we want to build. In our case, we are going to build a decision tree model, so this distribution is definitely not a problem, since decision tree models do not make assumptions with regards to the distribution of variables. However, if we were building a statistical model, which does have assumptions regarding variable distribution, we could potentially run into some problems.

To visually assess the relationship between the fields Num_persons_worked and Income_category, we will continue to use the **Histogram** node:

1. Edit the **Histogram** node.
2. Click the **Color** drop-down arrow.
3. Select the field Income_category, as shown in the following screenshot:

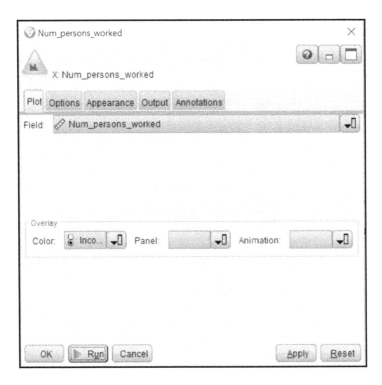

4. Click the **Options** tab.
5. Click **Normalize by color**.
6. Click **Run**:

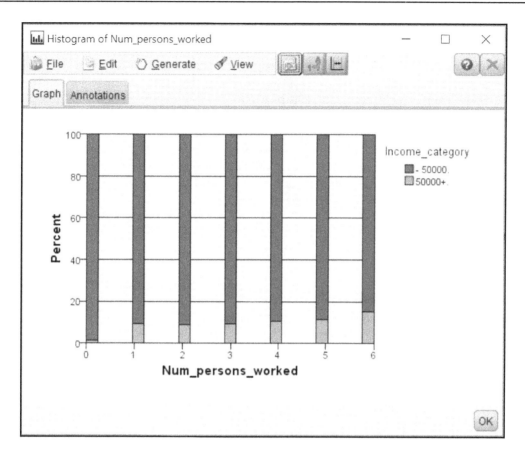

As before, the **Normalize by color** option allows us to better see the relationship between fields. This relationship does not seem as strong as what we previously observed in the earlier example. Nonetheless, it seems as though lower values are associated with less income and higher values are associated with more income. In order to quantify this relationship, however, we need to use the Means node.

Means node

When analyzing data, you are often concerned with whether groups differ from each other. The Means node allows us to determine if two groups differ significantly on a continuous variable. Specifically, the Means node compares the mean differences between independent groups or between pairs of related fields to test whether a significant difference exists. For example, prior to modeling, it would be useful to investigate whether there are significant differences between income categories based on the continuous fields we are planning to use as predictors. This node calculates a one-way analysis of variance based on the selected fields. In cases where there are only two groups, the results are essentially the same as an independent sample t-test. To use the Means node:

1. Place a **Means** node from the **Output** palette on the canvas.
2. Connect the **Type** node to the **Means** node.
3. Double-click on the **Means** node to edit it.

By default, the option **Between groups within a field** compares the means for independent groups within a field. The **Between pairs of fields** option is used to compare the mean values of two related fields. For example, you could compare the same person's income from one year to the next to determine if there is a change. When this option is used, the node calculates a paired-sample t-test on all pairs of fields you define. The **Options** tab allows you to set threshold p values used to label results as `Important`, `Marginal`, and `Unimportant` (or you can use other labels if you prefer).

In this example, we will test for mean differences between the two categories of income and the three continuous fields, `Age`, `Num_persons_worked`, and `Weeks_worked`, which we will use in our model. To do this:

1. Click the **Fields** list button in the **Grouping field** list and select `Income_category`.

2. Click the **Fields** list button in the **Test field(s)** list button and select `Age`, `Num_persons_worked`, and `Weeks_worked`, as shown in the following screenshot:

3. Click **Run** and you will get the following result:

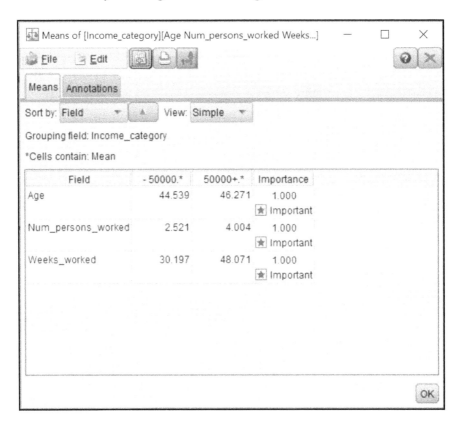

The cell values under each income category are the group means within the field in the left column. For example, the mean weeks worked for people in the less than $50,000 income category is 30.2, and for those in the more than $50,000 income category the mean weeks worked is 48.1. The Importance column indicates that the group means differ significantly on the field. In this instance, the probability value for the field is 0.0 (rounded off). It would appear that this field should be included in a model predicting the income category.

4. Click the **View** drop-down arrow and select **Advanced**, as shown in the following screenshot:

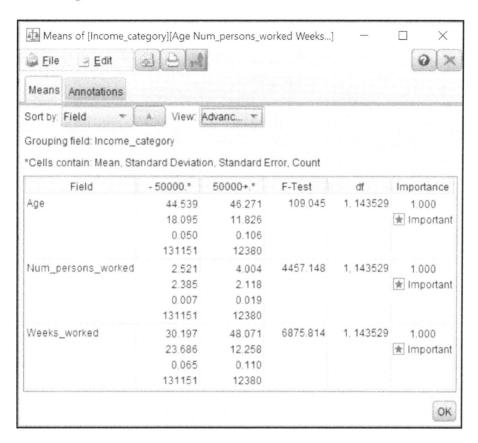

The **View** option allows you to specify the level of detail you want displayed in the results. The **Simple** view displays only the cell means and importance values in the output. The **Advanced** view also includes the **Standard Deviation**, **Standard Error**, **Count**, the **F-Test** value, and the degrees of freedom (**df**).

Relationships between continuous fields

This section examines and quantifies the relationship between two continuous variables. The Plot and Statistics nodes will be discussed over the next few pages. Ideally, we would investigate the relationship between the outcome field and a predictor, however the target field in our dataset is not a continuous variable, therefore we will look at relationships among predictors in the following examples.

 Note that it can be extremely important to investigate relationships among predictors so as to avoid problems like multicollinearity (extreme overlap among predictor variables that creates unstable solutions), but also to choose among similar predictors in terms of practicality or cost-effectiveness.

Plot node

The Plot node shows relationships between continuous fields. The Plot node allows users to visually check the relationship between two continuous fields by creating a scatter plot. A scatter plot displays individual observation in an area determined by a vertical and horizontal axis, each of which represent the variables of interest. To create a scatter plot:

1. Place a **Plot** node from the **Graphs** palette onto the canvas.
2. Connect the **Type** node to the **Plot** node.
3. Edit the **Plot** node.

To see the relationship between two continuous fields, place a field in each field option:

1. Click the **X field** drop-down arrow.
2. Select the field Age.
3. Click the **Y field** drop-down arrow.

4. Select the field `Num_persons_worked`, as shown in the following screenshot:

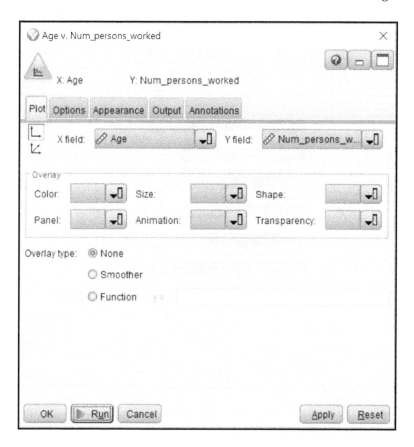

5. Click the **Options** tab.
6. Select **Sample**.

7. Click **Run**. You will get the following result:

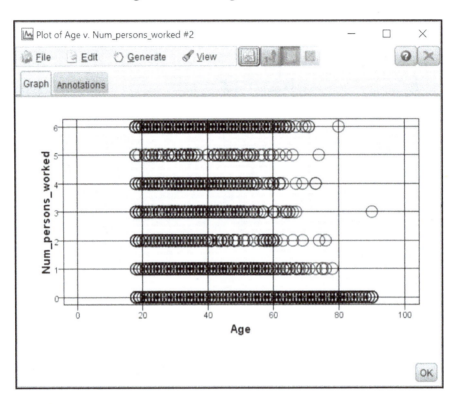

We have now created a scatter plot showing the relationship between age and the number of people that work. Notice that this is not a very strong relationship, because it is a bit difficult to see a clear relationship or pattern, however it does seem that to a certain extent, high values in one field tend to be associated with low values in the other field. In order to quantify this relationship, we need to use the Statistics node.

Statistics node

The Statistics node provides summary statistics for individual fields and correlations between fields. Whereas a scatterplot visually depicts the relationship between two continuous variables, the Pearson correlation coefficient is used to quantify the strength and direction of the relationship between continuous variables. The Pearson correlation coefficient is a measure of the extent to which there is a linear (straight line) relationship between two variables. Assessing correlation coefficients allows researchers to determine both the direction and strength of this relationship.

The correlation coefficient measures the extent to which two continuous fields are linearly associated. The correlation value ranges in value from -1 to +1, where +1 represents a perfect positive linear relationship (as one field increases the other field also increases at a constant rate), and -1 represents a perfect negative relationship (as one field increases, the other decreases at a constant rate). A value of zero represents no linear relationship between the two fields.

 One limiting aspect of using correlations is that they only give you an indication of linear relationships between continuous fields. Relationships between fields need not be linear, however, and these nonlinear relationships can be extremely important. Therefore, be careful not to discard fields too quickly.

To use the Statistics node:

1. Place a **Statistics** node from the **Output** palette on the canvas.
2. Connect the **Type** node to the **Statistics** node.
3. Double-click on the **Statistics** node.

The Statistics node produces summary statistics and provides correlations between fields. In this example, we will ask for summary statistics for all the continuous fields that we will use in the model, and then we will see how they relate to each other.

Correlations between the fields selected in the **Correlate** list and those selected in the **Examine** list will be calculated:

1. Click the **Examine** field list button and select Age, Num_persons_worked, and Weeks_worked.
2. Click **OK**.
3. Click the **Correlate** field list button and select Age, Num_persons_worked, and Weeks_worked.

4. Click **OK**. You will get the following result:

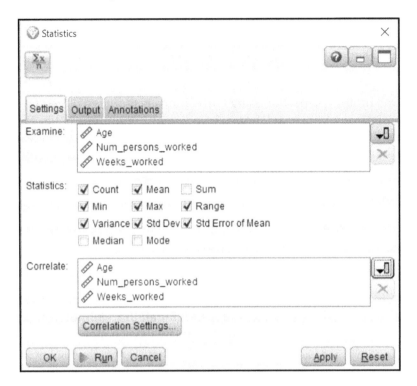

The **Correlation Settings...** dialog defines what it considers to be weak or strong relationships, and the level of importance is equal to *1-p* value (the *p* value is the significance value calculated by a statistical test). By default, an importance value below 0.90 is considered Unimportant, between 0.90 and 0.95 is labeled Marginal, and values greater than 0.95 are labeled Important. You can change these settings if you wish.

5. Now, click **Run**.

Along with the descriptive statistics, the report displays the correlation between each pair of selected fields (each field selected in the **Correlate** field list, with each field selected in the **Examine** field list), as shown in the following figure. The report also suggests how to interpret the strength of the linear association between the fields, according to the definitions set within the **Correlation Settings...** button:

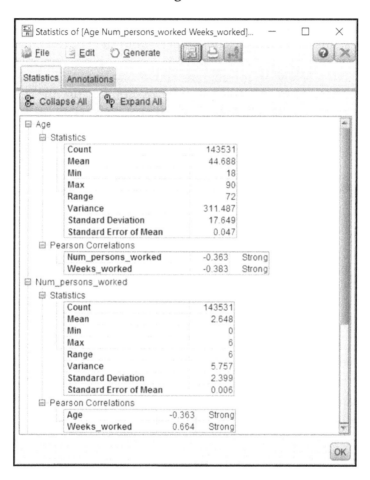

Scrolling through the output, we can see that the number of people who worked had a strong positive correlation with the weeks worked (0.664), while all the other relationships in this example were negative and only moderate (-0.363 and -0.383).

It is important to look at the actual correlation coefficients themselves and not just the labels that are provided by Modeler. By default, any correlation that is statistically significant will be labeled as `Strong`, but this label does not imply that the relationship is substantively or practically important.

As an aside, students always ask what a strong relationship is, and the honest answer is that this depends on your field of research. For example, in social sciences, where often there are multiple factors involved in predicting behavior, correlations above .30 are considered great, but in hard sciences correlations below .90 are not very useful. Therefore, it is important to be familiar with your area of research to really understand the significance of your findings.

Summary

This chapter focused on discovering a simple relationship between an outcome variable and a predictor variable. You learned how to use several statistical and graphing nodes to determine which fields are related to each other. Specifically, you learned to use the Distribution and Matrix nodes to assess the relationship between two categorical variables. You also learned how to use the Histogram and Means nodes to identify the relationship between categorical and continuous fields. Finally, you were introduced to the Plot and Statistics nodes to investigate relationships between continuous fields.

In the next chapter, you will be introduced to the different types of models available in Modeler and then provided with an overview of the predictive models. Readers will also be introduced to the Partition node so they can create training and testing datasets.

9
Introduction to Modeling Options in IBM SPSS Modeler

The previous chapter focused on exploring simple relationships between an outcome variable and a predictor variable. You learned how to use several statistical and graphing nodes to determine which fields are related to each other, and as mentioned previously, this can answer very important questions. However, ultimately you will want to build a model. In this chapter, you will be introduced to the different types of models available in Modeler and will then be provided with an overview of the predictive models. Specifically, in this chapter we will:

- Provide an overview of the kinds of models that Modeler can create and how these are organized
- List and discuss the various algorithms that Modeler organizes under classification
- Discuss the Auto nodes
- Discuss how to choose a model

This chapter will not be a theoretical grounding of all possible modeling techniques found in statistics and machine learning. There is no shortage of books that attempt this, but this book is focused solely on IBM SPSS Modeler, and therefore, we are only interested in the wealth of options in Modeler. A single chapter cannot demonstrate or even describe all of the modeling options in detail, so we have a more modest goal. We will attempt a kind of taxonomy of the available techniques.

The idea is that if you have a general sense of what is possible, and can identify a modeling technique that will likely be useful to you, then you can begin the process of learning more about it. Even in this high-level discussion, we won't exhaustively list all of the algorithms, but we will describe more than a dozen of the more important modeling nodes in this chapter. `Chapter 10`, *Decision Tree Models*, will be an important companion to this chapter, in that, we will take a single modeling approach, decision trees, and show you how modeling works in Modeler. Another valuable source of information is one of the software documentation user guides, *IBM SPSS Modeler 18.0 Modeling Nodes* (`ftp://public.dhe.ibm.com/software/analytics/spss/documentation/modeler/18.0/en/ModelerModelingNodes.pdf`). This document is nearly 400 pages long, longer than this entire book, and discusses each node in considerable detail. We hope that this orientation will get you started, and you won't have to revisit this topic in more detail until you are ready.

In a sense, the Modeler interface gives us a head start in developing our taxonomy—the **Modeling** palette has tabs on the left-hand side that help to organize the many options. We will use this as a starting point, but for greater clarity we will subdivide some of the larger categories. The nodes in the **Analytic Server** tab, will not be discussed in this chapter because most users of SPSS Modeler will not need nor have access to these functions. They are used to run predictive models on big data sources using technologies such as Spark and Hadoop:

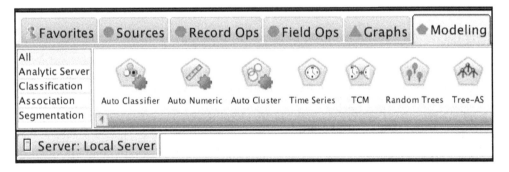

Modeler has dozens of modeling nodes, but they can be usefully organized into the following main approaches:

- **Classification**
- **Association**
- **Segmentation**

Classification

The main idea behind Classification is that you are trying to predict or understand one variable by making use of other variables. For example, you may be trying to predict which customers are likely to apply for a credit card, and you are trying to predict this from the customers' demographic and financial variables. Hence, in this scenario there are two types of variables:

- **The target variable**: This is a variable that you are trying to predict or understand
- **The input variables**: These are variables that you are using to try to predict or understand the target variable

The ultimate goal of this type of analysis is predictive accuracy. In this course, we will only have time to cover a couple of predictive models. Modeler offers a great number of predictive models. This section gives an overview, distinguishing between three classes of classification models, which are listed as follows:

- Rule induction models
- Statistical models
- Machine learning models

Rule induction models are an important type of predictive model. All of these models derive a set of rules that describe distinct segments within the data in relation to the target. The model's output shows the reasoning for each rule and can therefore be used to understand the decision-making process that drives a particular outcome. Models that produce decision trees belong to this class of models.

Modeler offers a number of traditional statistical prediction models. These models produce equations, and statistical tests guide predictor selection. In order to do so, these models make certain assumptions whereas rule induction and machine learning models do not make assumptions.

Machine learning models are optimized to learn complex patterns. No assumptions are made such as those made by traditional statistical techniques. Machine learning models do not produce a set of rules as rule induction models do and are often said to be black box models. These models will produce a set of equations, but because there is a hidden layer (and there can be more than one hidden layer), the interpretation of the weights is not straightforward, as with traditional statistical models or rule induction models. Ultimately, these models are used for their predictive accuracy, but not for understanding the mechanics behind a prediction.

As you will see in the next few paragraphs, classification is a broad topic—one where the outcome field's level of measurement is extremely important—therefore, it is necessary to further subdivide predictive modeling based on the types of level of measurement of the target field.

Categorical targets

Modeler combines a wide variety of techniques in the **Classification** tab of the Modeling palette. The following figure shows some of the methods for just one subset. These techniques can be used for classification with a categorical target variable. The three rows in the figure further represent three subsets for this type:

- Rule induction and decision trees
- Statistical classifiers
- Machine learning classifiers

Categorical target classifiers in Modeler

CHAID, **Quest**, **C5.0**, and **C&R Tree** (first row) all produce the familiar tree diagram, which we will explore in some detail in the next chapter. Of all the algorithms in Modeler these are probably the most generally applicable and the easiest to learn. If you are new to Predictive Analytics, you should master at least one of these first. **Decision List** is similar to decision trees, in that it also generates rules, but does not produce the tree diagram.

Also, while rules in trees are always mutually exclusive, rules in **Decision List** do not need to be. For both of these reasons all five can be referred to as rule induction techniques, but only four of the five are considered decision tree techniques. Finally, **Decision List** has an interesting feature, wherein you can manually encode business rules and then ask the algorithm to add them to the list that you provide. Of the rule induction models, the most commonly found outside of Modeler are **CHAID**, **C5.0**, and **C&R Tree**. Users of other platforms and languages are most often familiar with at least one of these (even if they don't know them by name). Also, books on this subject will tend to mention at least one of these. Therefore, choosing to learn one of these algorithms first is a good idea.

Discriminant analysis and **Logistic Regression** (in the second row) are very common techniques drawn from multivariate statistics. There are hundreds of books that discuss them, but mastering them usually requires at least some familiarly with statistics. If that describes your data analysis background, then adopting how they are used in Modeler will probably not be that difficult. If you are new to statistics, you might want to start with decision trees instead because some of the model output produced by these two statistical techniques may be unfamiliar to you and you may not possess all of the prerequisite knowledge for using them.

Many of the hot algorithms, popular in courses and in books, come from the machine learning tradition (the third row in the previous figure). **Random Trees** is a kind of averaging across many trees. It can be very powerful but you lose the advantage of those wonderful tree diagrams because you can't produce a diagram for a collection of trees. **Neural Net** are experiencing a bit of a renaissance in light of the success of deep learning to perform tasks such as driverless cars and speech recognition. These neural nets are not *deep*—meaning simply that they are not as complex, but deep learning often requires enormous amounts of data, often millions of observations.

The **Neural Net** in Modeler, most often **Multi-Layer Perceptrons** (**MLP**), can be excellent classifiers, but there is a competency to develop, so it is best to learn a bit of the theory about them first. **Support vector machines** are another popular machine learning technique. They have the reputation of being able to better handle short and wide datasets, meaning datasets that have a lot of inputs and not a huge number of cases. They also have a skill set associated with them and you will need to tune them, which means that you will have to adjust the settings to develop a good model. **K-nearest neighbors** (**KNN**), is a lazy algorithm in that no model is built per se, instead, the algorithm searches the historical data and tries to make a prediction based on similar cases that it finds in the data and the outcomes associated with these cases.

Numeric targets

Many of the same algorithms that we've seen so far can also be used for numeric targets, where you are trying to predict something like a dollar amount or another continuous value. There is an easy way to keep track of which algorithms are used for categorical targets only, numeric targets only, or both. If you look at the **Expert** tab in an Auto node like the **Auto Numeric** node you can see a list of the algorithms that can be used to make the kind of prediction shown in the following screenshot. We will discuss all three Auto nodes in more detail in the next section:

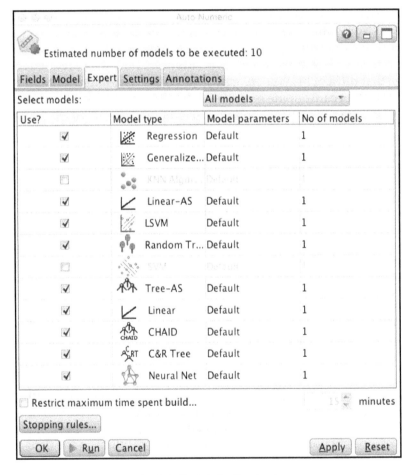

Numeric classifiers in the Auto Numeric node

Notice that **CHAID** and **Neural Net**, among others, appear in this list and also appeared listed in the previous section. They can be used with either categorical or continuous targets. Notice also that **Regression** and **Linear** appear in this list, but they did not appear in the previous list. This is because they can only be used to perform numeric target predictions. So the best way to remember is to check both in this node and the **Auto Classifier** node to see what is available. It is recommended to learn at least one categorical classifier and one numeric classifier before you start to use the Auto nodes.

Linear Regression is the most famous of these algorithms. If you are already familiar with regression, then the **Regression** node will be closer to what you are expecting. It is the *plain vanilla* regression you would encounter in a university setting. The **Linear** node has some impressive features, but does a lot behind the scenes. It will discard weak variables and perform other kinds of automatic data preparation for you. It might be a good idea to develop a familiarity with the advanced features of the **Linear** node before you trust it to run without oversight. Even when its settings are consistent with your goals, you will want to understand what it is doing.

The Auto nodes

The basic idea behind the Auto nodes is that they allow you to run many different models. These models are then ranked on some criteria and then the chosen models are combined into a kind of committee called an ensemble. Previously, we have seen the **Expert** tab of the **Auto Numeric** node. The **Auto Classifier** node, for example, produces a predictive model for categorical classification, and success is defined as making accurate predictions. This might seem obvious, but it is only true for the **Auto Classifier** whether we are right or wrong. When predicting a mortgage default, for instance, the model predicts default and the customer does, indeed, default. With the **Auto Numeric** model, on the other hand, we might predict that a customer is going to spend $517.80, and the actual spend turns out to be $516.12. Most of us would consider that a pretty good prediction, yet it failed to be completely accurate. This doesn't pose a problem, but we will need different criteria than accuracy.

The **Auto Classifier** can run more than a dozen models, rank them on overall accuracy (or your choice from some other criteria) and picks the top three (by default). Then, it proceeds to combine all three into a kind of committee, called an ensemble, and it is the ensemble that is recommended by the **Auto Classifier**. An **Auto Numeric** model also picks the top three models (by default), but the criterion is different. It uses criterion such as the size of the error (there are other choices), and then it also forms an ensemble.

Finally, the **Auto Cluster** model uses a generally accepted criterion for a good cluster solution, called silhouette. It is rare to create an ensemble while doing clustering, so it is probably the least used of the three Auto nodes. The most effective way to use the **Auto Cluster** model would be to get some indication of which solution might be best, followed by building an individual model.

Data reduction modeling nodes

There are some modeling nodes in the **Classifier** tab that are not really classifiers at all, and might not be quite what you expect modeling nodes to be. The reason they are in this tab is that they support your modeling efforts. The reason that they are considered modeling nodes is that they produced a diamond or nugget when they are run. All nodes that do this will have a pentagon shaped icon and will be considered modeling nodes even if they don't produce a model in the form of an equation such as regression or a set of rules such as a decision tree. Two examples are particularly important and will be discussed here: **Feature Selection** node and **Factor/PCA** node.

It is the job of the **Feature Selection** node to help you choose the most useful inputs. Some modeling techniques benefit from an initial screening of inputs before running the model. This is especially true of modeling techniques that use every input in the final model. Neural nets are an example of models that benefit from predictor reduction. Other modeling techniques (such as decision trees) only use a subset of the input variables that are provided, and in a sense, perform their own feature selection. **Feature Selection** uses three basic criteria to eliminate fields: the ability to predict the target, the amount of missing data, and the amount of variance. Variables with little or no variance are not very useful in the final model. Once the **Feature Selection** node runs, it produces a model, which acts as a filter, allowing only the stronger variables to flow to any of the downstream modeling nodes.

If you have a background in statistics, you have almost certainly encountered factor analysis and principle components analysis. These techniques are often less familiar to those with backgrounds in machine learning. The basic idea behind these techniques is to find relationships among, and possible redundancy in, the collection of input variables, with the goal of reducing the number of inputs. Therefore, it has a similar goal as the **Feature Selection** node, but goes about it in a radically different way. It is rarely the end goal of a Modeler project to perform a factor analysis. This model is typically used in service of a larger goal. The resulting model produces factor scores, which can be used instead of the original inputs, and the number of factors will always be smaller than the original number of inputs.

Modeler users, draw upon their knowledge of the data and the results of a factor analysis to better understand their data, but do not necessarily have to replace the original inputs with the derived factors. The whole topic of data reduction, which includes both **Feature Selection** and factor analysis is a big topic. There are a handful of data reduction tips and tricks in the *IBM SPSS Modeler Cookbook* by *Packt*.

Association

As consumers, most of us have encountered recommendation engines where a movie is recommended based upon prior viewing habits or books are recommended based upon prior purchases (or even based simply on prior viewing behavior). Association Rules analysis is often described primarily as kind of market basket analysis, but while it is strongly associated with retail data it can be applied in other areas. For example, in the area of predictive maintenance, a pair of part failures might be frequently associated with a third part failure even though the third part has not yet shown evidence of trouble. Modeler supports three different **Association** nodes: **Apriori**, **Carma**, and **Association Rules**.

The fourth algorithm, **Sequence**, is a bit different. It takes either the time-date stamp, or a simple ranking in time, into account. The transactions in Association Rules often occur at the same time. For instance, on a receipt at a grocery store many items might be listed. Hot dogs and hot dog rolls might frequently occur together, but the rules do not indicate that either purchase came before the other in time. In fact, one would expect rules to indicate both that hot dogs predict rolls and vice versa. Sequence analysis does, however, make a distinction between pairs of items that occurred in a different sequence. It too can be useful in predictive maintenance or in web mining. In web mining, it might be the sequence in which clicks occurred or which pages were accessed and read. All four nodes in the **Association** tab are shown as follows:

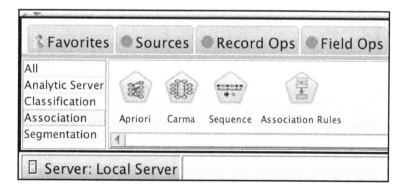

The Association tab

Segmentation

Segmentation (as shown in the following screenshot) is very different from **Classification**. With segmentation or clustering, the main idea is that you do not believe that all the cases in the dataset are similar. That is, you believe there are distinct groups of people, and these groups should be looked at separately. Often, cluster analysis is used in marketing campaigns so that not all customers receive the same ads, but instead receive the appropriate ads. In this scenario, there is no dependent variable, only independent variables that are used to segment the cases.

K-means is the oldest of the techniques and has been popular and widely available for decades. It uses the distances between cases (on scale variables only) to determine similarity. Here, distance can be thought of quite literally—Euclidian distance is a common method. Cases whose values are close on the scale variables are grouped into clusters in an attempt to find homogeneous subsets. Determining how many clusters to create is part of the challenge of such techniques. Since the clusters are exploratory in nature, these analyses are not right or wrong in the same sense that predictive models are. They should be judged by their utility in addressing the business problem.

The **Kohonen** node and the **TwoStep** node are variations on a theme. Kohonen Networks were originally described by Teuvo Kohonen, who called them self-organizing maps. They are a specialized neural network for producing unsupervised segmentation. **TwoStep** extends the idea of **K-means** into new territory. It allows for categorical variables and makes an attempt to determine how many clusters provide for an optimal solution. **Anomaly** detection also builds on the notion of **K-Means** by measuring the distance from the cluster centers or centroids. The cluster center represents the average values of a cluster so that a case that is distant from the cluster center is therefore unusual and might merit review—such cases might be erroneous data or possibly might even be indicative of fraud:

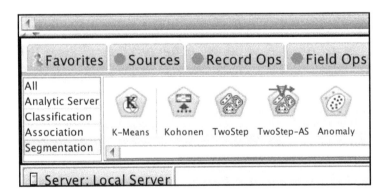

The Segmentation tab

Choosing between models

Obviously, if you have a field in the data that you want to predict, then any of the classification models (depending on the target field's measurement level) will perform the task, with varying degrees of success. If you want to find groups of individuals that behave similarly on a number of fields in the data, then any of the clustering methods is appropriate. Association Rules are not going to directly give you the ability to predict, but are extremely useful as a tool for understanding the various patterns within the data.

But if you want to go further and decide which particular technique will work better, then unfortunately the answer is that it depends on the particular data you are working on as well as your business goals. It is going to be important to remember that all models have a different perspective on data when it comes to:

- How missing values are handled
- How continuous predictors are handled
- How categorical predictors are handled
- How a model scores data

So, there are many subtle differences between the models. In the end, it is always the business user, balancing all the pros and cons, who decides which model should be used. Or, maybe the user decides to run multiple models, and combine them into one single overall model. Again, there is a wide range of possibilities, and it is only the business user who can decide what to do.

The advantage of Modeler is the simplicity of building the models. Neural networks, rule induction (decision trees), and statistical models can be built with great ease and speed, and their results compared. You must remember that data mining is an iterative process: models will be built, broken down, and often even combined before the user is satisfied with the results.

One final yet important point to keep in mind when building models is that Modeler will only find rules or patterns in data if they exist. You cannot extract a model with high accuracy if no associations between the fields exist. However, in Tom Khabaza's nine laws (`http://khabaza.codimension.net/index.htm`), in the so-called Watkins Law, David Watkins makes the following claim:

> *There are always patterns.*

This law was first stated by David Watkins:

We might expect that a proportion of data mining projects would fail because the patterns needed to solve the business problem are not present in the data, but this does not accord with the experience of practicing data miners.

What the law is getting at is that if we are analyzing our customer data it is inevitable that there will be clues in the data about our customer's behavior. Now that we've arrived at the modeling phase, if your model fails to find meaningful patterns, what do you do? What Watkin's law teaches us is if we fail to find associations between our input fields, then we likely have to return to an earlier phase, particularly the data preparation phase, to revisit opportunities that we've missed because relevant patterns should be there, but the modeling algorithms can only utilize what we give them.

Summary

This chapter provided an overview of the different kinds of models available in Modeler. You were also introduced to the various types of predictive models that can be used. In addition, the Auto Modeling nodes were discussed. Finally, there was a section that focused on how to choose a model.

In the next chapter, we will discuss the logic behind decision tree models. We will also go through a detailed example of how to use the **CHAID** model, as you will become familiar with its theory, dialog boxes, and how to interpret its results.

10
Decision Tree Models

The previous chapter provided an overview of the various types of data mining models (predictive, clustering, and association) that can be developed in Modeler. Predictive modeling is the most common form of data mining, and as was mentioned in the previous chapter, three very different strategies can be employed: statistical, decision tree, or machine learning. In this chapter, we will discuss:

- Decision tree theory
- **CHAID** theory
- Partition node
- **CHAID** dialog options
- **CHAID** results

Before we begin discussing decision tree theory, we'll look at a brief overview of where the next two chapters are going. In this chapter and the next, we are going to build a classification model using **Chi-square Automatic Interaction Detection** (CHAID). We will then assess its ability to make effective predictions, and finally use the model to score new cases. Our teaching experience has shown us that in order to limit confusion, it is a good idea to briefly revisit the notion of an algorithm and contrast it with a model. In the previous chapter, we reviewed numerous algorithms; these included **CHAID,** but there were many other algorithms, including some that have similar goals to **CHAID,** such as **C&R Tree** and **C5.0.** An algorithm is a systematic step-by-step process for solving a problem. **CHAID** is an example of an algorithm. It uses input variables and a target variable to establish a formulaic relationship between those inputs and the outcome. That formula, a decision tree model, can then be used to score future data. In the world of Modeler, the algorithms always have a pentagon shape, and the resulting model is always a diamond shape.

Many new practitioners of predictive analytics get concerned when two different models seem to disagree. Often our colleagues and management get concerned as well. Two algorithms can disagree in a number of ways. They can:

- Select different predictors
- Have different levels of accuracy
- Make different predictions for the same case
- Produce different-looking formulas
- Score some cases as missing while other models provide a score

These differences are not just occasional experiences—they are often the case. Only in the case of a trivially small and uncomplicated dataset will two different algorithms completely agree. If you focus too much on surface-level differences, you will lose confidence in the process. If you dig deeper, you will typically see that multiple models produced on the same data will agree with each other much more often than they disagree. Part of the art of predictive modeling is learning when two models are so different as to cause concern, which prompts you to favor one over the other, and when two models are telling a similar story about the data.

What might be even more surprising is that two **CHAID** models might disagree with each other, even on the same project. There are a few reasons why this might happen:

- Even if the original data is the same, there might be something different about the stream or the type node that is being fed into the **CHAID** modeling algorithm
- Two models might have a different defined partition
- The **CHAID** settings might be different

It is important to note that this is not necessarily a cause for concern. It is very likely that you intended that they be different. For instance, as we will see in this chapter, you might purposely build a **CHAID** model with a setting of 95% confidence and another with a setting of 90% confidence. In a real-world project, it is very common to build as many as a half dozen or more variations using the very same modeling algorithm, thereby creating several generated models (diamonds shaped nodes) using just a single modeling node (pentagon shaped). We will revisit the concept of two different generated models disagreeing with each other in the next chapter. For now, keep in mind that our motivation for reviewing this at the start of this chapter is so that you understand why you would be motivated to adjust **CHAID's** setting.

Decision tree theory

Decision or classification trees are extremely common predictive models that successively partition data based on the relationship between the target and predictor variables. Decision tree models indicate which predictors are most strongly related to the target. These methods are capable of combing through a large set of predictors by successively splitting a dataset into subgroups on the basis of the relationships between predictors and the target field. Decision tree models classify cases into groups and predict values of a target field based on the values of the predictor fields.

Decision trees have some very attractive features:

- They create segments that are mutually exclusive and exhaustive, meaning that they allow you to identify homogeneous groups
- They make it easy to construct rules for making predictions about individual cases
- They can handle a large number of predictors, so that the most important variables are at the top of the tree and the least important variables are not used at all
- They can handle interactions
- They can handle non-linear relationships
- They have very few assumptions

The following image is an example of a decision tree. The base of the tree is known as the root node. It shows you the distribution of the entire sample. Here we can see that 45,865 people have an income of less than $50,000 and 4,319 people have an income of more than $50,000. In this example, the most important predictor is the `Educated_fulltime` field because this is the field that created the first split. Notice that the `Educated_fulltime` field had two values, so the tree split on these values (if this field had had more than two values, the tree would split based on whichever values of the field were different from each other—it may be that all the categories differ from each other or only some of them). Notice that the `Educated_fulltime No` group had no additional splits; therefore this is a Terminal node—that is, it is a node that gives us a prediction. In this case, the prediction is that people with a value of `No` on the `Educated_fulltime` field will have an income of less than $50,000. This prediction was applied to 43,599 cases and it was accurate 95.3% of the time. For those that had a value of `Yes` on the `Educated_fulltime` field, their data was then further split by the `Investment` field.

For those `Yes Educated_fulltime` people that had no investments, they were predicted to have an income of less than $50,000. This rule was applied to 3,832 cases and it was accurate 77.7% of the time. Finally, for `Yes Educated_fulltime` people that had investments, they were predicted to have an income of more than $50,000. This rule was applied to only 2,753 cases and it was accurate 51.4% of the time. In this example, the tree-depth, the number of levels below the root node, was two levels:

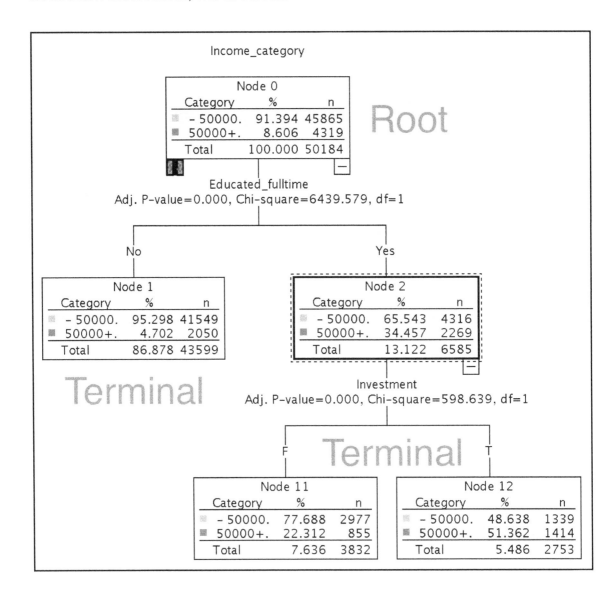

Modeler contains a number of different algorithms for performing rule induction: **C5.0, CHAID, Quest, C&R Tree** (classification and regression trees), and **Decision List**. They are similar in that they can all construct a decision tree by recursively splitting data into subgroups defined by the predictor fields as they relate to the target field; however, there are important differences among these methods. In this chapter, we will only focus on the **CHAID** model.

CHAID theory

CHAID is a decision tree model. It is one of the oldest and most popular data mining techniques. At its core, **CHAID** is based on the Chi-square test; it chooses the predictors that have the strongest interaction (give the largest Chi-square statistic) with the target field and then it divides the sample based on this predictor. It can use the Pearson or Likelihood ratio Chi-square statistic. In the figure shown next, notice that the `Educated_fulltime` field is the most important predictor, because this is the field that has the largest Chi-square statistics. In fact, notice that the Chi-square statistic and percentages are exactly the same for both the **CHAID** model and the Chi-square test. In addition, if the categories of the predictor do not differ significantly from each other, the categories will be merged together. **CHAID** generates non-binary trees so it tends to create wider trees:

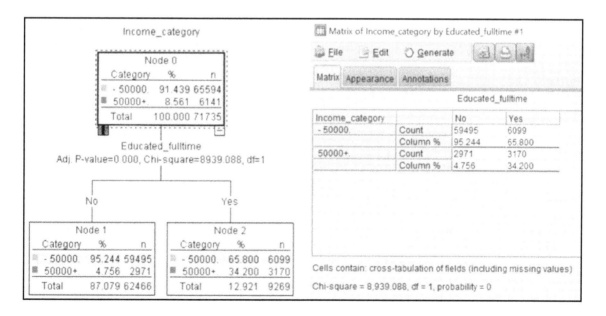

How CHAID processes different types of input variables

When using **CHAID,** or any algorithm, it is critical that you properly declare the level of measurement for your input variables. This includes properly declaring variables that do not belong in the analysis at all, the so-called `Typeless` inputs. The reason that level of measurement is so important at this stage is that **CHAID** will treat the different kinds of input in quite different ways. In this section, we will discuss how **CHAID** handles different types of input. On occasion, you may even choose to be a little creative about how you declare them. For instance, on real-world projects, it is not uncommon for analysts to take a variable that is clearly an ordinal variable, such as `Income_category`, and experiment with declaring it as nominal in order to force **CHAID** to apply a different approach. This trick is a bit advanced, and should be done with caution, but it underscores why it is important to understand what the modeling techniques are doing under the hood.

CHAID utilizes the Chi-square statistic for both selecting variables, and in performing merges. Merges are an important concept. **CHAID** will automatically group categories within inputs that are not significantly different from each other. In this way, **CHAID** will only form a complex branch when it makes sense to do so. This prevents the tree from becoming overly complex with lots of little leaf nodes with small sample sizes. Merging is the primary way that CHAID treats the various levels of measurement differently.

When **CHAID** encounters a nominal input, it will determine whether any of the separate and distinct categories fail to be significantly different from each other. Any category can be combined with any other category. So if `Education Level` is declared as a nominal input, PhDs can be combined with the `Less Than High School` category. However, if `Education Level` is declared as an ordinal variable, different rules will apply. `Education Level` is a good example because it is not always clear whether a variable like this is ordered. For instance, a PhD and an MD have a similar amount of schooling. You have to know your input and the history from data collection to data preparation to make the best determination. When in doubt, it is probably best to declare this variable as a nominal.

When **CHAID** encounters an ordinal variable, it will also collapse non-significant categories, but only if those categories are contiguous. So if an input such as number of children is considered, cases with one and two children might be combined, but cases with one child will not be combined with five or more children unless all categories between one and five were also collapsed into one node. This is also a good example because one could make a reasonable case that number of children is a continuous variable. Note that in our case study dataset, some of our inputs are string variables and only numeric variables can be declared as ordinal.

If you really know statistics, you may know that the Chi-square test is designed only for categorical variables and not for continuous variables. Yet **CHAID** utilizes the Chi-square test, so how does it use continuous variables? It uses a fairly clever trick. It bins the continuous variables into deciles, and then proceeds to treat them like ordinal inputs. It does the job nicely, but the potential shortcoming is that the cut-points between the deciles are essentially arbitrary and those are the only cut-points that are considered. So although **CHAID** will collapse contiguous deciles that are not significantly different, don't expect **CHAID** to identify extremely precise cut-points.

CHAID has a very easy-to-understand approach to missing data. Unlike some other algorithms (such as **C&R Tree)** that have fairly complex routines for handling missing values, **CHAID** simply leaves them alone. It treats missing data as its own category. Imagine that you have some folks that do not have a recorded age. The resulting branch might simply have four nodes: `< 40`, `40-65`, `65+`, and `missing`. As an added feature, when the missing cases are similar (not significantly different) to another group then they are sometimes collapsed with them. For this reason, **CHAID** can be an interesting choice during data understanding. While it would be too early at that stage to produce a model, using **CHAID** to simply explore a very preliminary model can inform you as to the severity of any issue regarding missing data and something of the characteristics of your missing data.

Stopping rules

There are three primary stopping rules that indicate when it is time for **CHAID** to stop growing a decision tree. These stopping rules will be briefly mentioned again when presenting the applicable **CHAID** settings:

- **Tree depth**: This is how deep (or tall) the decision tree is allowed to grow. The default setting is five levels, meaning that the tree will stop after five layers of branches have grown below the root node, even if there are still inputs capable of making a significant split.
- **Significance**: We've discussed how significance plays a role in how variables are merged. Once the optimal merge is determined for each input, **CHAID** looks for the best input to use for a split. It will be the input that has the lowest p value (significance statistic) of all of the available input.

- **Minimum node size**: **CHAID** has special thresholds for how many cases have to be in both a parent node and a child node. If a node does not meet the parent threshold, a split will not be considered at all. It is also the case, however, that the resulting child nodes must meet the child node sample size requirement. This prevents a decision tree from becoming too granular in detail—in such cases, a very complex tree that appears to be accurate on the train data, is likely to overfit and perform poorly on test (and new) data.

All three of these rules exist to avoid overfitting, a subject that we will revisit in its own section later in the chapter.

Building a CHAID Model

Here's how you would build a **CHAID** Model:

1. Open the Ready for Modeling stream.

   Once you have completed all of your data preparation, there are still a couple of things that need to be done before you can begin to build your models. First of all, you need to make sure that all of your data is instantiated (fully read). This is crucial because all fields need to be instantiated before any model can use them. It is also useful at this point to specify within the Type node, the different roles each field will play in the models. As a reminder, within the Type node, the field to be predicted must have its role set to **Target**. All fields to be used as predictors must have their role set to **Input**. Any field that will not be used in the model must have its role set to **None**.

2. Edit the **Type** node.
3. Make sure that the following fields have their roles set to None, as they will not be used in our current model: Occupation, Industry, and Education.
4. Click **OK.**

Finally, let's look at the **Partition** node.

Partition node

The **Partition** node is a very important node in Modeler. The **Partition** node simply creates a special `Partition` field that can be used directly by modeling nodes. This way, rather than literally creating two data sets, Modeler allows you to retain one data file that is split into two (or three) sets. One set is used for training, another for testing. This is extremely important, because this way models are developed on the training data, and then tested on new (testing) data. This then serves as a test of reliability (replication) so that we can better trust our results, and it makes it less likely that we are capitalizing on chance. It also provides some peace of mind that what we have found is a real result that will generalize to new data:

1. Edit the **Partition** node.

The **Partition** node is found in the **Field Ops** palette. It generates a `Partition` field that divides the data into separate subsamples for the training, testing, and validation stages of model building. By default, the node randomly selects 50% of the cases for training purposes and reserves the other 50% for testing the model. These proportions can be altered (for example, 70% for training and 30% for testing is a common split):

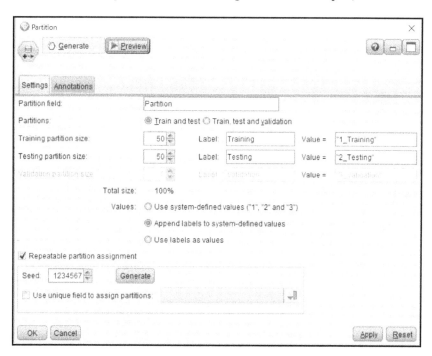

The **Partition** node generates a categorical field with the role set to `Partition`. The default name of the field is `Partition`. One very nice aspect of the Partition node is that models will only be developed on the `Training` dataset, yet predictions will automatically be made for records in the `Testing` (and `Validation`) samples as well as the `Training` dataset. The sizes (in percentages) of the three partitions can be set with the controls. The percentages should add up to 100%.

The **Repeatable partition assignment** option allows you to duplicate the same results in another session. Specifying the starting value used by the random number generator ensures that the same records are assigned each time the node is rerun:

1. Click **OK**.

   To demonstrate the effect of the **Partition** node, let's request a **Table** node to look at the records.

2. Add a **Table** node to the stream.
3. Connect the **Partition** node to the **Table** node.
4. Run the **Table** node, then scroll to the last column (not shown).

Notice that the new `Partition` field has been added to the data and has values of `1_Training` and `2_Testing`.

Overfitting

Overfitting is arguably one of the most treacherous risks you face when building predictive models. This happens when the performance on the train data looks great (maybe too good), but the performance on the test data is much worse. We will have more to say about diagnosing overfitting in the next chapter, but we need to discuss ways of avoiding it now. In earlier chapters, we saw how to reclassify variables with a large number of categories into variables with fewer categories. These inputs with many categories are dangerous. The reason that they can lead to overfitting is that, despite large sample sizes, there may be only a handful of cases that have a rare combination of traits. Let's explore just two examples of this phenomenon in the dataset.

There are 622 PhDs in `Train` dataset. Of that number, the most common occupation is `Professional Specialty` with 396 PhDs in that specialty. A rare occupation within this group is `Transportation and Moving materials`. There are just two of them, neither of whom is earning more than $50,000. In contrast, in the `Test` data, 50% of this combination meet that threshold. Importantly there are also only two of them! Watch out for those rare categories that have 100% or 0% splits. They distract the algorithm in that the tree will want to split at those extremes and then when applied to new data, that part of the tree will fail.

Let's consider just one more rare combination. Professional degrees are not common in the dataset, but they are not rare either. There are 870 of these in the `Test` dataset. However, only 8 of those 870 have `Precision craft and repair` as their occupation. Twenty-five of those eight are in the higher income target category. In the `Test` data, the percentage is 75%. What may be tricky to understand at first is that we are not especially interested in the `Test` data, per se. We are interested in the danger to which it alerts us. We are not going to deploy our model on the `Test` data. We are going to deploy our model on new data that we don't have yet, and that possibly does not exist. It is data from the next year, and the years after that. But the `Test` dataset is acting like a canary in a coal mine and it is warning us that we are about to overfit the model. This kind of detailed analysis of each and every rare combination would be a very clumsy way to detect overfitting. We will be learning a more efficient approach in the next chapter using the **Analysis** node. For now, the important lesson learned is to watch out for data that might be too granular and might represent small sample sizes hiding away in rare combinations of variables:

1. Place the **CHAID** node from the **Modeling** palette on the stream canvas.
2. Connect the **Partition** node to the **CHAID** node.

The name of the **CHAID** node should immediately change to `Income_category`, since this is the target.

CHAID dialog options

Let's take a look at the options within the **CHAID** modeling node:

1. Edit the **CHAID** node.

   The **Fields** tab indicates how each field will be used in the model. The default is to **Use predefined roles** from the Type node; however, you can choose **Use custom field assignments** to make modifications:

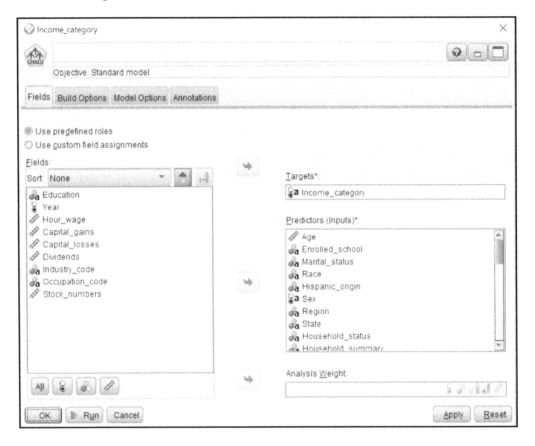

2. Click the **Build Options** tab:

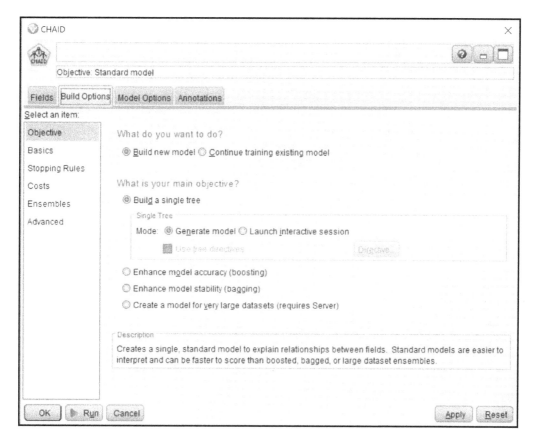

The **Build Options** tab is where you set up all the options for building the model. Lets take a look at the options:

- **Build new model** creates a completely new model each time you run a stream.
- **Continue training existing model** continues training the last model successfully produced by the node.
- **Build a single tree** creates a single, standard decision tree model.
- **Mode** specifies the method used to build the model. **Generate model** creates a model automatically when the stream is run. **Launch interactive session** opens the tree builder, which enables you to build your decision tree as you specify predictors.

- **Enhance model accuracy (boosting)** works by building multiple models in a sequence. The first model is built in the usual way. Then, a second model is built in such a way that it focuses on the records that were misclassified by the first model and so on. Finally, cases are classified by applying the whole set of models using a weighted average.
- **Enhance model stability (bagging)** creates multiple models and combines them, in order to obtain more reliable predictions.
- **Create a model for very large datasets (requires Server)** divides the data into smaller data blocks and builds a model on each block.

3. Click the **Basics** submenu.

Let's take a look at the options in this menu:

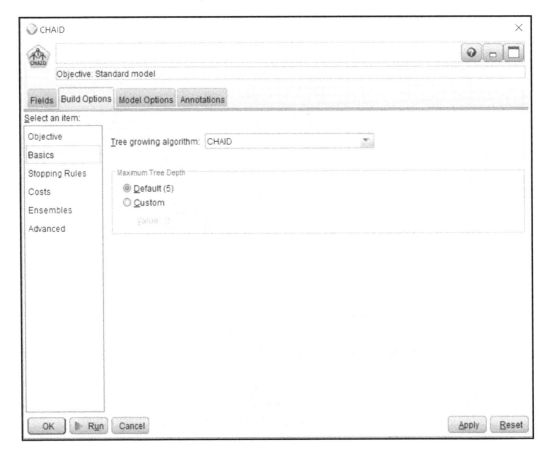

- There are two decision tree algorithms for this model: **CHAID** and **Exhaustive CHAID** (a modification of **CHAID** that examines all possible splits for each predictor).
- **Maximum Tree Depth** controls the maximum number of levels of growth beneath the root node.

4. Click the **Stopping Rules** submenu:

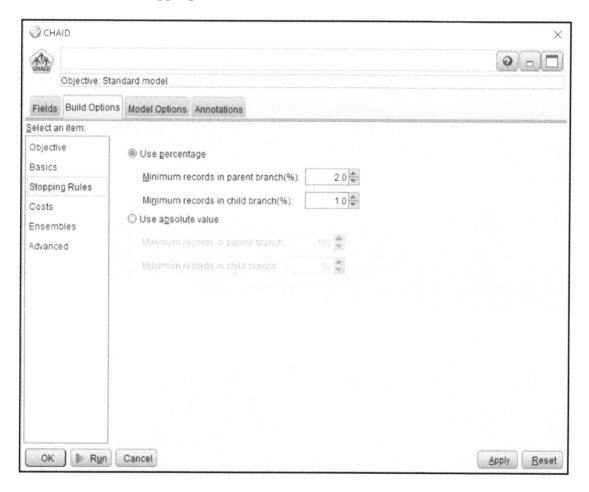

This submenu controls the minimum numbers of cases for nodes, and this can be set as an absolute value or as a percentage of cases. Nodes that do not satisfy these criteria will not be split.

5. Click the **Costs** submenu:

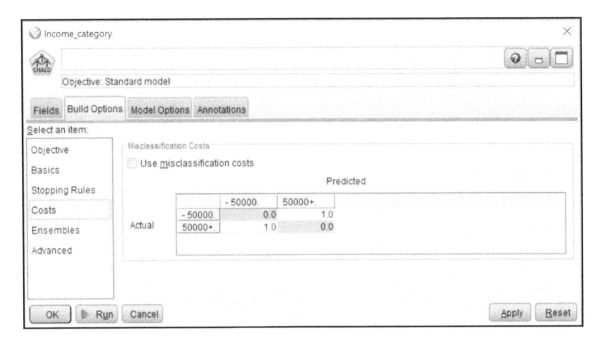

For categorical target fields, **Misclassification Costs** allow you to include information about the relative penalty associated with incorrect classification. The default is that all misclassifications have equal weight; however, you can specify that certain classifications are costlier.

6. Click the **Ensembles** submenu:

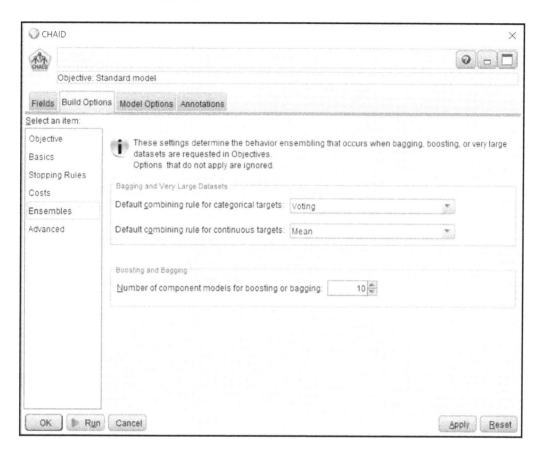

These settings determine the behavior when combining models for boosting, bagging, or very large datasets, which are requested in the **Objective** tab:

- **Bagging and Very Large Datasets**: When scoring an ensemble, this is the rule used to combine the predicted values from the base models to compute the ensemble score value
- **Boosting and Bagging**: Specifies the number of base models to build when the objective is to enhance model accuracy or stability

7. Click the **Advanced** submenu:

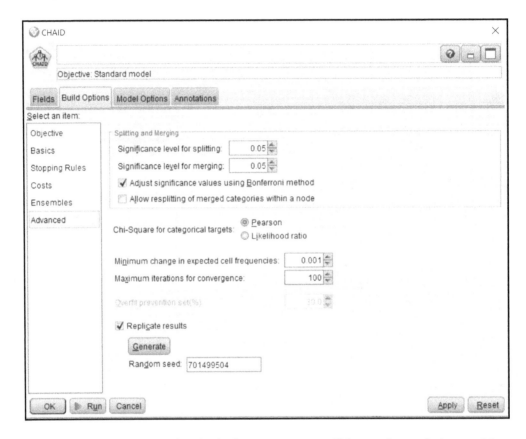

This submenu controls which chi-square test will be performed along with corresponding significance levels:

- **Significance level** controls the significance value for splitting nodes and merging categories.
- **Adjust significance values using Bonferroni method** is for when you are making multiple comparisons; the significance values for merging and splitting criteria are adjusted using the Bonferroni method.
- **Allow resplitting of merged categories within a node** allows the procedure to re-split merged categories if that provides a better solution.

- **Chi-Square for categorical targets** specifies which Chi-square test you want to use.
- **Minimum change in expected cell frequencies** must have a value greater than 0 and less than 1. Lower values tend to produce trees with fewer nodes.
- **Maximum iterations for conergence** stops the tree from growing because the maximum number of iterations has been reached. You may want to increase the maximum or change one or more of the other criteria that control tree growth.

8. Click the **Model Options** tab:

This menu calculates predictor importance and propensity scores:

- **Model name** generates the model name automatically based on the target field or you can specify a custom name.
- **Calculate predictor importance** produces an appropriate measure of importance, so you can display a chart that indicates the relative importance of each predictor in estimating the model.
- **Propensity Scores (valid only for flag targets)** calculates propensity scores (predicts the likelihood of a true value). Raw propensity scores are derived from the model based on the `Training` dataset only. Adjusted propensities attempt to compensate by looking at how the model performs on the test or validation partitions.

9. Click **Run**.
10. Edit the generated **CHAID** model.

CHAID results

Two panes are visible in the **CHAID** model window. The pane on the left contains the model in the form of a decision tree. Initially, only the first branch of the tree is visible. The other pane contains a bar chart depicting variable importance, which is a measure that indicates the relative importance of each field in estimating the model. Since the values are relative, the sum of the values for all fields on the display is 1.0. Notice that the `Educated_fulltime` field is the most important field in this model. The next most important field is `Investment`, followed by the `Sex` field. Also notice that only the fields that were used by the model were kept:

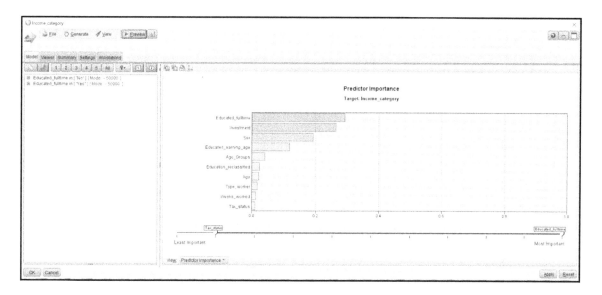

The `Educated_fulltime` field creates the first split in the tree. This information is saying that if `Educated_fulltime` has a value of `No`, then mode value for `Income_category` is less than $50,000. The Mode lists the most frequent category for the branch, and the mode will be the predicted value, unless there are other fields that need to be taken into account within that branch to make a prediction.

You can click number **2** to see the second level of the decision tree, and then click number **3** to see the third level of the decision tree, and so on.

1. Click the **All** button to expand the rules.
2. Click the **%** button to see the numeric values:

This first rule says the following:

People that have a value of No on the Educated_fulltime field, and do not have investments, and work in either Federal government or Self-employed-incorporated, and are females, the model predicts will have an income of less than $50,000. This rule applies to 723 cases and the accuracy of that rule is 95.9%! On the other hand, if these people have a value of No on the Educated_fulltime field, and they do not have investments, and they work in either Federal government or Self-employed-incorporated, but are males, the model still predicts that they will have an income of less than $50,000; however, this rule applies to 815 cases but the accuracy is only 82.1%. So even though the prediction was the same as the first group, the confidence in the prediction is much lower.

So for these people, with no college education and who are not working full-time, with no investments, and working either for Federal government or on their own, it seems that gender has an impact in terms of their likelihood to have an income less than $50,000. Why might this be? Is it that women with the same qualifications as their male counterparts are being paid less? Or is there another reason? Remember it is always necessary to compare the predictions of a model with both previous models and knowledge and experience about the specific problem.

If you would like to present the results to others, an alternative format is available in the **Viewer** tab that helps visualize the decision tree:

1. Click the **Viewer** tab.

The root of the tree shows the overall percentages and counts for the two categories of Income_category. The modal category is shaded in each node. The first split is on the Educated_fulltime field, as we have seen in the text display of the tree. Similar to the text display, we can decide to expand or collapse branches. In the right corner of some nodes, a+ or a- is displayed, referring to an expanded or collapsed branch, respectively. To hide (collapse) all nodes in a branch click the minus sign (-) in the small box below the lower-right corner of the node. To show (expand) the nodes in a branch beneath a node, click the plus sign (+) in the small box below the lower-right corner of the node.

The next figure only shows the six nodes below the root. It can be interesting to see the distribution of responses in a node. If we expand each of the Investment nodes, we can see additional levels:

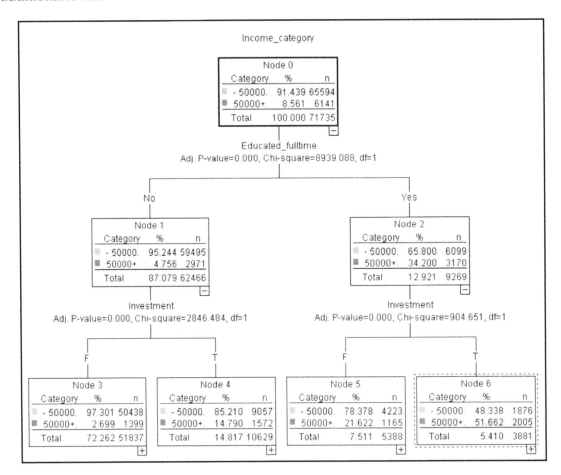

We see that for people in Node 3, the next most important field is Type_worker, whereas for people in Node 4 the next most important field is Sex, and so on. You can then see the distributions within each node and you can further expand each node to understand the complete rules.

In the **Viewer** tab, toolbar buttons are available for showing frequency information as graphs and/or as tables, changing the orientation of the tree, and displaying an overall map of the tree in a smaller window (treemap window) that aids navigation in the **Viewer** tab.

As a side note, we can now start to get an appreciation for how different models are structured. Statistical models, such as logistic regression, create an equation that applies to all the cases and all the variables, so it is very easy to see the one unit impact of anything. Decision tree models, such as **CHAID,** create many rules where only some of the fields apply to some of the cases.

Let's view the results of the model in a table:

1. Connect the generated **CHAID** model to the **Table** node:

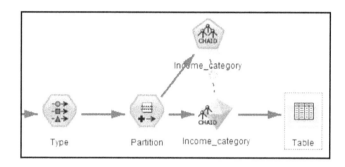

2. Run the stream:

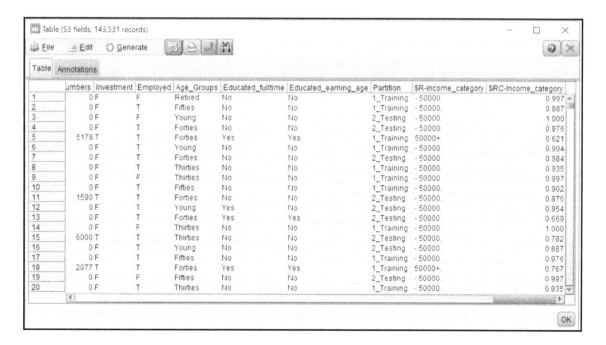

The $R-Income_category field contains the most likely prediction from the model. The probabilities for the target categories must sum to 1; the model prediction is the category with the highest probability. The probability value is contained in the $RC-Income_category field. So for the first case, the prediction is -50000 and the predicted probability of this occurring is 0.997 for this combination of input values. Ideally, you want the probability value to be as close to 1 as possible. Also notice that predictions have been made for both the Training and Testing datasets (even though the model was only built on the Training dataset).

During this chapter, we did not demonstrate any steps to reduce the data before building the model. Why not? Decision tree techniques, such as **CHAID,** often do a pretty good job without a data reduction step, but you should be cautioned against assuming that is always the case. An algorithm such as a neural network is prone to overfit, since it does not perform data reduction prior to building the model, therefore, it is important to know your algorithm. In light of what you have learned in this chapter, you might want to return to the section on the data reduction nodes in the previous chapter. What if we did need to perform data reduction? We might consider trying the following:

- You could use either the **Feature Selection** node or the **factor/PCA** node, both of which are briefly discussed in the previous chapter. Watch out when trying to use **Factor/PCA** on this dataset, however, as **factor/PCA** is used for continuous variables and we have mostly nominal variables in this dataset.

- You could build a decision tree, and then examine the inputs that were utilized by the decision tree and feed only the selected input to a neural net algorithm. This is actually a popular and powerful trick but can fail to take advantage of the way a neural net views data.

- You could use a variety of advanced techniques that involve finding the best combinations of variables while reducing the total number of variables. The Packt *IBM SPSS Modeler Cookbook* dedicates more than half a chapter (more than almost any other single problem) to a variety of advanced tips and tricks for data reduction.

Summary

This chapter discussed in detail the theory behind decision tree models, and **CHAID** in particular. Various important issues regarding the model building process were discussed, and readers became familiar with the dialog boxes and results of the **CHAID** model.

In the next chapter, we will continue to develop our model building skills by comparing models using the **Analysis** and **Evaluation** nodes. Readers will also learn how to score new data and how to export those predictions outside of Modeler.

11
Model Assessment and Scoring

In the previous chapter we built a model. In this chapter, we are going to discuss different ways of assessing and improving the results of a model. In addition, you will also begin to learn how to use your models in the real world. Specifically, we will cover the following topics:

- Contrasting model assessment with the **Evaluation** phase
- Model assessment using the **Analysis** node
- Modifying CHAID settings
- Model comparison using the **Analysis** node
- Model assessment and comparison using the **Evaluation** node
- Scoring new data
- Exporting predictions

Contrasting model assessment with the Evaluation phase

As we briefly discussed in `Chapter 1`, *Introduction to Data Mining and Predictive Analytics*, model assessment (a modeling phase task) is quite different from the **Evaluation** phase. Some of the same tools can apply to both, but the stage of the project and the thought process is quite different. During model assessment, you are potentially comparing a large number of models. You may even try dozens of variations of algorithms, settings, and modifications to the data.

Therefore, you need easy, objective criteria on which to rank these models. Our colleagues and management simply will not have the time to be brought in to judge the efficacy of dozens of models so we need to narrow it down to just a couple of models before the **Evaluation** phase begins. Tom Khabaza, one of the original authors of CRISP-DM has written the *Nine Laws of Data Mining* (`http://khabaza.codimension.net/index_files/9laws.htm`) and the *8th Law of Data Mining* is the *Value Law*, which states:

> *The value of data mining results is not determined by the accuracy or stability of predictive models.*

Well, in this lesson, particularly in the **Analysis** node section, we are going to focus on the accuracy and stability of a model. So, what is this law getting at? An extended quote will help make the distinction:

Accuracy and stability are useful measures of how well a predictive model makes its predictions. Accuracy means how often the predictions are correct (where they are truly predictions) and stability means how much (or rather how little) the predictions would change if the data used to create the model were a different sample from the same population. Given the central role of the concept of prediction in data mining, the accuracy and stability of a predictive model might be expected to determine its value, but this is not the case.

The value of a predictive model arises in two ways:

1. *The model's predictions drive improved (more effective) action.*
2. *The model delivers insight (new knowledge), which leads to improved strategy.*

So the important thing here is that when we move beyond model assessment and into evaluation, we have to shift our focus from accuracy and stability to action and strategy. We need an intervention strategy that uses our predictions to drive action. The **Evaluation** phase will be to measure, as specifically as possible, how the improved actions produced measurably better results. Better is usually measured in dollar terms, but not always. So, we have to return our project to the language of the business and compare our performance to the specific goals laid out in the **Business Understanding** phase.

Model assessment using the Analysis node

When a model seems satisfactory based on performance, fields included, and the relationships between the predictors and the target, the next step is model assessment. Formally, model evaluation is the assessment of how a model performs on unseen data. Modeler makes this easy because of the `Partition` field.

We previously used the **Partition** node to split the data file into `Testing` and `Training` partitions. In the previous chapter, we were careful when studying the model not to use the `Testing` partition. Doing so would compromise model testing because we would learn how well the model performed on the unseen data. In this chapter, we will use the **Analysis** and **Evaluation** nodes to further assess our model.

The **Analysis** node allows you to evaluate the accuracy of a model, and it organizes output by the `Partition` field values. **Analysis** nodes perform various comparisons between predicted values and actual values for one or more generated models. The **Analysis** node is contained in the **Output** palette:

1. Open the `Assessment` stream.
2. Add an **Analysis** node from the **Output** palette.
3. Connect the generated CHAID model to the **Analysis** node.
4. Edit the **Analysis** node:

The **Analysis** node provides several types of output. **Coincidence matrices (for symbolic targets)** are cross tabulations between the predicted and actual values. The **Confidence figures (if available)** option provides summary information for models that produce confidence values.

By default, the **Analysis** node will organize output by the Partition field. We can also ask that all the output be broken down by one or more categorical fields:

1. Click **Coincidence matrices (for symbolic targets)**.
2. Click **Run**:

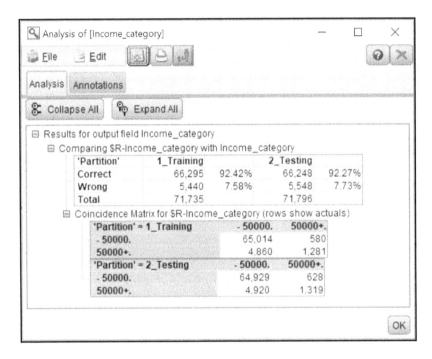

The table shows the overall accuracy of the model in the Training and Testing partitions. When we were examining the CHAID model, we only saw information on the Training dataset and rule specify accuracy; here we are provided with the overall model accuracy.

As we can see from the output, the overall accuracy of the CHAID model on the `Training` data is 92.42%. Whether this level of accuracy is acceptable will depend on many factors. More important is how well the model performed on the unseen `Testing` dataset. The accuracy of the CHAID model for the `Testing` group is the fundamental overall test of the model. If the accuracy on the `Testing` data is acceptable, then we can deem the model validated.

For this data , the `Testing` dataset accuracy is 92.27%. The typical outcome when `Testing` data is passed through a model node is that the accuracy drops by some amount. If accuracy drops or changes by a large amount (about 5%), it suggests that the model overfit the `Training` data or that the validation data differed in some systematic way from the `Training` data (although the random sampling done by the **Partition** node minimizes the chance of this). If accuracy drops or changes by only a small amount, it provides evidence that the model will work well in the future; that is, we have a reliable model that will generalize to new data. When this is favorable, the model is described as being stable. The small change of 0.15% in accuracy from the `Training` to the `Testing` data indicates that the CHAID model is validated.

In summary, we are focused on two questions:

- Is the test accuracy value sufficiently high
- Is the stability sufficient—as revealed by a small difference between train and test accuracy

The Coincidence Matrix table will be of special interest when there are target categories in which we hope to make accurate predictions. We can calculate the accuracy for each group. For the −50000 group in the `Testing` partition, the accuracy is *(64929/(64929+628))*100=99.04%*. For the 50000+ group in the `Testing` partition, the accuracy is *(1319/(1319+4920))*100=21.14%*. Again, we need to determine whether this level of accuracy is acceptable.

Note that these percentages can be automatically calculated using a **Select** node to split the data based on the partition field and then using a **Matrix** node to calculate the relationship with observed and predicted values.

One's first reaction might be that we naturally want all of our predictions, in both categories, to be accurate. While this is true, there are circumstances where one of the categories takes on special significance. If you were trying to predict whether a case would or wouldn't have a serious illness, you might want to be particularly focused on finding cases with the illness even at the risk of making some errors in the form of false positives. It is not an issue with our case study data set, but it is why the Coincidence Matrix and an ability to interpret it can be important. If the model is doing an excellent job with one outcome category, but a poor job with the other, it always deserves a careful look.

If the model is acceptable the way it is, great; if it needs to be improved, one approach is to modify the algorithm that was used (we will do this next), and another approach is to build another model using a different algorithm. A final strategy is that we can go back to the **Data Preparation** phase and further prepare the data. You can also combine models, but that is beyond the scope of this book.

Modifying CHAID settings

It might seem surprising to cover changing settings in this chapter since we built the model in the previous chapter, but during model assessment we are still in the **Modeling** phase of CRISP-DM. Also, you are typically changing model settings in response to something positive and encouraging that you see (or fail to see) in the **Analysis** node results. The defaults are generally good, and should be used first, but there is always room for improvement.

Previously we had discussed two main criteria in the **Analysis** node—the accuracy on the Test data and the ability to generalize from Train to Test. While there are a large number of settings that you can change in CHAID, nearly half of them have something to do with these criteria, accuracy, and generalizability.

In our discussion of Modeler's essentials, we will explore only those settings that directly affect this trade-off. The basic concept is simple. If you want greater accuracy, build a bigger tree. By adding branches, and more leaf nodes, you will inevitably increase the accuracy on the Train data but be careful what you wish for because you may be disappointed when you check the accuracy on the Test data. If you push too hard and overfit the model, than you will have the situation that we discussed previously—the gap between the Train performance and the Test performance will be unacceptably large.

So, the solution, again, is easy. If you want a tree that generalizes better, make a smaller tree. When you make the tree smaller, the overall accuracy will inevitably go down but you will eventually achieve the result you desire, which is bringing that gap in performance to within acceptable limits. The following table shows some of the settings that you can choose and their effect on tree size:

	Larger tree—greater accuracy but risk overfitting	Smaller tree—less accurate but improved generalizability
Maximum tree depth	Increase	Decrease
Minimum records in parent and child branch	Decrease	Increase
Significance level for splitting and merging	Consider 0.1 for 90% confidence	Consider 0.01 for 99% confidence
Bonferonni adjustment	Turn off (very real risk of overfitting)	Leave it checked (safer)

Lets build a second CHAID model where we modify the default settings. To do this:

1. Place a second **CHAID** node onto the stream canvas.
2. Connect the **Partition** node to the second **CHAID** node.
3. Edit the second **CHAID** modeling node.
4. Click the **Build Options** tab.
5. Click the **Basics** submenu.
6. Change the **Maximum Tree Depth** value to 10.
7. Click the **Stopping Rules** submenu.
8. Click **Use absolute value**.
9. Type 200 in the **Minimum records in parent branch** option.
10. Type 100 in the **Minimum records in child branch** option.
11. Click **Run**.

The modifications that we just made will allow the decision tree to become larger. In essence, we are trying to improve model accuracy, without compromising generalizability; we previously had seen that the model was stable:

12. Edit the second generated **CHAID** model.

Notice that the tree-depth is only eight levels instead of the ten levels that we had requested. Given that we did not reach the maximum number of levels requested, this means that either there were no additional rules or some of the other previously mentioned stopping rules (for example, minimum records in parent or child branches) were triggered.

Also notice that the variable importance order has changed, but not by much, as several of the variables we created are still among the top predictors. Finally, if you look at the first two rules, these are exactly the same as the ones we had previously found:

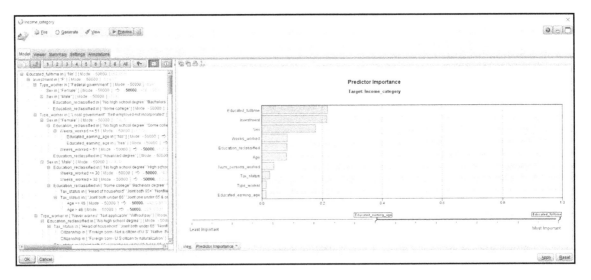

1. Click OK.

Model comparison using the Analysis node

The Analysis node can also be used to directly compare the performance of two or more models. When two models are placed in the same stream, they can be jointly assessed with an Analysis node. Before we do this, let's take a quick look at each model's predictions:

1. Connect the second generated **CHAID** model to the first generated **CHAID** model.
2. Connect the second generated **CHAID** model to the **Analysis** node.

3. Connect the second generated **CHAID** model to the **Table** node:

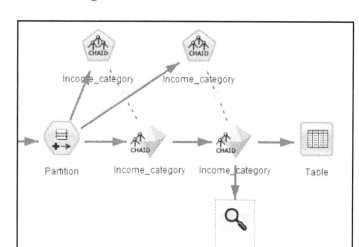

This places both models on the same steam so you can compare them.

4. Run the **Table** node:

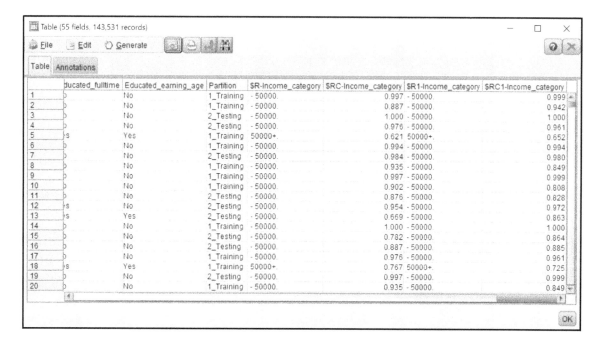

You can now see the predictions of each model. Notice that for the first twenty rows both models are making the same predictors; however, the confidence values are different. Now we will compare model results with the **Analysis** node:

1. Edit the **Analysis** node.
2. Make sure **Coincidence matrices (for symbolic targets)** is selected.
3. Run the **Analysis** node:

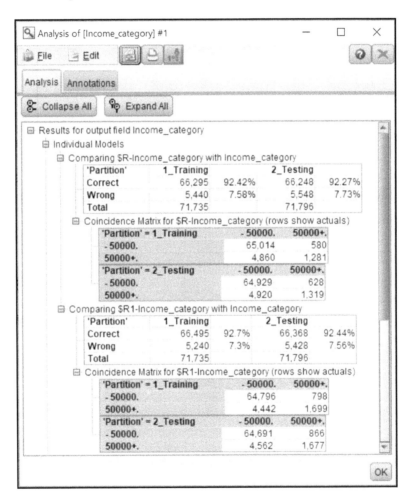

On the `Testing` partition, the first CHAID model is accurate on `92.27%` of the records, while the second CHAID model performs slightly higher on the `Testing` data (`92.44%`). Looking at the Coincidence Matrix for the `Testing` data, you can see that neither model predicts the `50000+` income category well; however, the second CHAID model does accurately predict 358 more `50000+` cases than the first CHAID model:

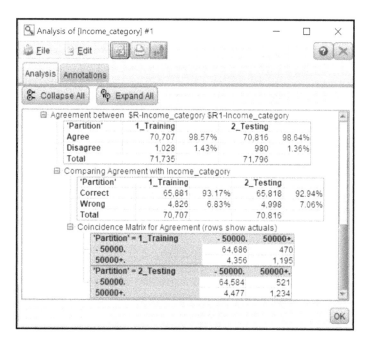

In this next set of tables, the first table shows how often predictions of the two models agree in both datasets. In the `Testing` partition, the models agree on `98.64%` of the cases. This is very high, meaning that the models are making very similar predictions.

The key question is, then, when the models agree, how accurate is the prediction? This is answered by the next table (`Comparing Agreement with status`), which shows that in the `Testing` partition, when the models agree, the two models are correct `92.94%` of the time. This is slightly better than the individual models by themselves. Still, every increase in inaccuracy can be important in a data-mining project, so if we wanted to combine these models there could be a slight increase in accuracy (however, rule interpretation would be much more difficult).

The third table (`Coincidence Matrix for Agreement`) shows predictions for each income category separately when the models agree.

Model assessment and comparison using the Evaluation node

The **Evaluation** node offers an easy way to evaluate and compare predictive models in order to choose the best model for your situation. Evaluation charts show how models perform in predicting particular outcomes. They work by sorting records based on the predicted value and confidence of the prediction, splitting the records into quantiles (groups of equal size), and then plotting the value of a criterion for each quantile, from highest to lowest.

Lets evaluate both models using the **Evaluation** node. To do this:

1. Place an **Evaluation** node from the **Graphs** palette onto the canvas.
2. Connect the second **CHAID** model to the **Evaluation** node.
3. Edit the **Evaluation** node:

- The **Chart type** option supports six chart types. Note that if the **Profit** or **ROI** charts are selected, then the appropriate options (**Costs**, **Revenue**, and record **Weight**) become active so information can be entered.
- The **Plot** drop-down menu controls the number of points plotted in a chart and the **Percentiles** choice will calculate 100 values, that is, one for each percentile from 1 to 100.
- The **Include baseline** option is useful as it indicates what a theoretical model predicts at the chance level.
- The **Include best line** option will add a line corresponding to a perfect prediction model—this is a theoretical model where predictions are always correct.
- The **Separate by partition** option provides an opportunity to test the model against the unseen data that was held out by the **Partition** node. If checked, an evaluation chart will be displayed for both the `Training` and `Testing` samples.

4. Click the **Include best line** checkbox.
5. Click **Run**:

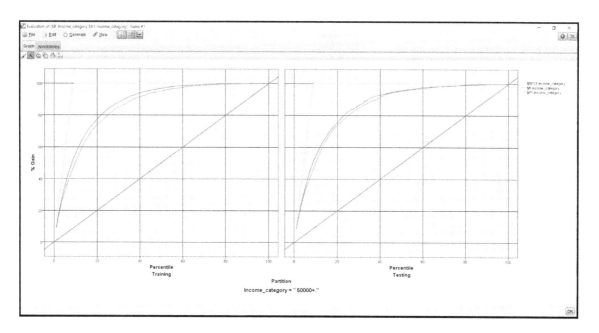

The gains chart is a way of visually evaluating how the model will do in predicting a specified outcome, in this case the `50000+` income group. Technically, the gains chart is a line chart of cumulative percentile gains, computed as: (*cumulative percentile targetn/totaltargetn*)*x 100* . Notice that the data is split by partition, so that we have a gains chart for both the `Training` and `Testing` datasets. One of the goals here is reliability, so we are looking for some consistency between the training and testing charts.

The vertical axis of the gains chart is the cumulative percentage of hits, while the horizontal axis represents the ordered (by model prediction and confidence) percentile groups. The diagonal line presents the base rate—that is , what we expect if the model is predicting the outcome at the chance level. Notice with the base line model, that as we have gone through the first 20% of the data (*x* axis), we have correctly identified 20% of the people with incomes greater than $50,000 (*y* axis). Likewise, when we have gone through the first 50% of the data, we have correctly identified 50% of the people with incomes greater than $50,000. In other words, we are just predicting at chance.

The upper line (labeled `$BEST-Income_category`) represents results if a perfect model were applied to the data. With this model, when we have gone through the first 5% of the data, we will have correctly identified 58% of the people with incomes greater than $50,000. In fact, once we go through the first 9% of the data, we will have identified 100% of the people with incomes greater than $50,000 and therefore the model flattens out because there are no additional cases to find. (Why 9%? Well, the people with incomes greater than $50,000 make up 9% of the `Training` dataset).

The two middle lines (labeled `$R-Income_category` and `$R1-Income_category`) display the results of our models. Notice that our models never follow the prefect prediction model closely (because our confidence values were never really high). All the lines connect at the extreme [`(0,0)` and `(100,100)`] points. This is because if either no records or all records are considered, the percentage of hits for the base rate, best model, and actual models are identical.

The advantage of a model is reflected in the degree to which the model line exceeds the base rate line for intermediate values in the plot. The area for model improvement is the discrepancy between the model line and the perfect model line. If our model line is steep for early percentiles, relative to the base rate, then the hits tend to concentrate in those percentile groups of data. At a practical level, this would mean for our data that many of the people with incomes greater than $50,000 could be found within a small portion of the ordered sample.

If you hold your cursor over the model line at any particular point, the percentage of hits is displayed. At the 20th percentile value on the horizontal axis, for example, we see that the second model produces 77% of the hits. This is an improvement over chance. In our case, it looks like the models performs similarly on both partitions and the second CHAID model had higher accuracy and confidence values (note that the second model extends further) than the first CHAID model.

A lift chart is another way of representing this information graphically:

1. Edit the **Evaluation** node.
2. Click the **Plot** tab.
3. Click the **Lift Chart Type** option.
4. Click **Run**:

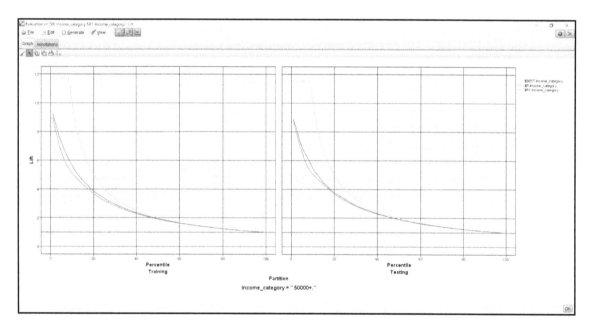

Lift charts plot a ratio of the percentage of records in each quantile that are hits divided by the overall percentage of hits in the dataset. Therefore the relative advantage of a model is expressed as a ratio to the base rate.

The vertical axis of the lift chart shows you how much better a model is compared to the base line model, while the horizontal axis represents the ordered (by model prediction and confidence) percentile groups. The baseline is at a lift of one because it is not an improvement over itself. The perfect prediction model is 11.68 times better than the baseline model for the first 9% of the data (again, in the `Training` dataset people with incomes greater than $50,000 made up 9% of the sample).

The middle lines display the results of our models. Notice that when looking at the first 9% of the data of the `Training` dataset, the second model is 5.91 times better than the baseline model.

Gains charts and lift charts are very helpful in marketing and direct mail applications, since they provide evaluations of how well a campaign would do if it were directed to the top X% of prospects, as scored by the model.

Again, it seems as though the model performs similarly on both partitions. Note that as a default, the **Evaluation** node graphs the results of the first category value, in this case people with incomes greater than $50,000. However, many times we will want to see the plots for the other category values as well. To view other values:

1. Edit the **Evaluation** node.
2. Click the **Gains Chart Type** option.
3. Click the **Options** tab.

To change the definition of a hit, check the **User defined hit** check box and then enter the condition that defines a hit in the **Condition** box. The Expression Builder can be used to build the expression defining a hit. This tab also allows users to define how scores are calculated, which determines how the records are ordered in evaluation charts. Typically, scores are based on functions involving the predicted value and confidence:

1. Click the **User defined hit** checkbox.
2. Click the **Condition** box type `@TARGET ="-50000.":`

Now we are going to display a gains chart for the people with incomes less than $50,000:

1. Click **Run**:

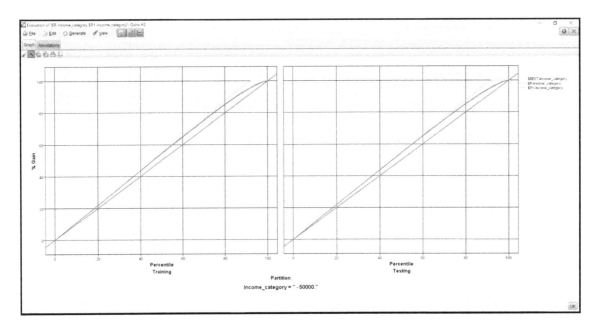

Again, it seems as though the models perform similarly on both datasets.

Scoring new data

Once a model is developed, whether it is a single model or a combination of models, it must be applied to new data to make predictions. In data mining, the act of using a model on new data is called deployment. There are many options for deploying Modeler models. In these final demonstrations, we will focus on how to score new records. It is important to note that scoring is only part of the **Deployment** phase, as deployment can be quite complex and can even involve migrating your model to a different software platform.

For instance, the IBM product **Collaboration and Deployment Services** (**C&DS**) is such a platform. Cloud based deployment in environments such as **Amazon Web Services** (**AWS**) is also possible. It is quite common to translate models (especially decision tree models) into another language such as SQL. There is even a special language, **Predictive Modeling Markup Language** (**PMML**) that is specifically designed for the purpose of migrating a model from one environment to another. Many companies, including IBM, are part of a group that supports PMML to facilitate this kind of collaboration between systems. All of this is under consideration during deployment because final deployment might involve automatically pulling new data nightly from a database and automatically populating an employee's screen to support a sales call. These complexities are beyond the scope of our *Essentials* guide, but serve to put scoring into a greater context.

Scoring is simply using our model (our model diamond) to calculate the model score on a record that was not present when the model was built. You do not need the modeling node for this part of the process; all you need is the generated model. It is helpful to reflect on the following fact—you can actually score a single record. You cannot build a model on a single record, but you can score one as we are simply plugging new values into a formula. To illustrate this process, we have created a typical deployment stream. Let's open and examine this stream:

1. Open the Scoring stream:

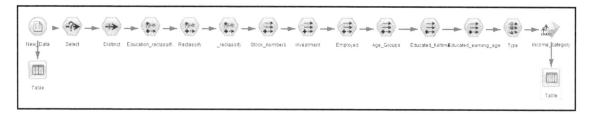

This stream contains only the essential nodes, including a source node for the data, **Select** and **Distinct** node to clean the data, **Reclassify** nodes to modify existing fields, **Derive** nodes to create new fields, a **Type** node to instantiate the data, and the second generated CHAID model (we will pretend this is the model we decided to keep). If we would like to use Modeler to make predictions on new data, this stream will be adequate.

Suppose that we are given new data and we want to make predictions on the `Income_category` field for each person. This new data has the same structure as the previous file. Of course, there is no `Income_category` field in this data file because that information is precisely what we want to predict.

2. Run the **Table** node at the beginning of the stream:

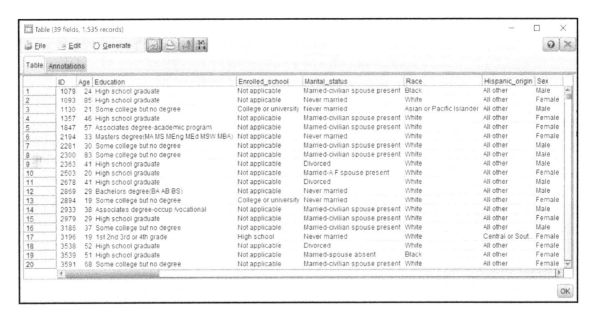

Notice that this is new data for only 1535 cases. Also, notice that there is no `Income_category` field in this data file. At this point, we are ready to make predictions for the new data. There is nothing special to do other than to run the data through the generated CHAID model. We'll look at the predictions with a **Table** node.

3. Run the **Table** node at the end of the stream:

	ntry_self_reclassify	Stock_numbers	Investment	Employed	Age_Groups	Educated_fulltime	Educated_earning_age	$R-Income_category	$RC-Income_category
1	ites	0 F	T		Young	No	No	- 50000.	0.999
2		0 F	F		Retired	No	No	- 50000.	0.979
3		0 F	F		Young	No	No	- 50000.	0.985
4	ites	0 F	T		Forties	No	No	- 50000.	0.948
5	ites	0 F	T		Fifties	No	No	- 50000.	0.961
6	ites	0 F	T		Thirties	Yes	No	- 50000.	0.794
7		0 F	T		Thirties	No	No	- 50000.	0.902
8	ites	0 F	F		Retired	No	No	- 50000.	0.981
9	ites	0 F	T		Forties	No	No	- 50000.	0.984
10	ites	0 F	T		Young	No	No	- 50000.	0.994
11	ites	1590 T	T		Forties	No	No	- 50000.	0.829
12	ites	0 F	T		Young	No	No	- 50000.	0.963
13		0 F	T		Young	No	No	- 50000.	0.999
14	ites	0 F	T		Thirties	No	No	- 50000.	0.849
15	ites	0 F	F		Young	No	No	- 50000.	0.999
16	ites	0 F	T		Thirties	No	No	- 50000.	0.849
17		0 F	F		Young	No	No	- 50000.	1.000
18	ites	2205 T	T		Fifties	No	No	- 50000.	0.982
19	ites	0 F	T		Fifties	No	No	- 50000.	0.994
20	ites	0 F	F		Sixties	No	No	- 50000.	0.999

New fields have been added to the data, including the model prediction ($R-Income_category), and the model confidence ($RC-Income_category). Model deployment can be as simple as this with Modeler. This type of deployment is often called batch scoring because we are making predictions for a group of records, rather than scoring individual records one at a time.

The trick to scoring is to make sure that all the fields are named exactly as they were when the model was created. This is because the generated model and any additional fields created are looking for fields named exactly what they were named initially.

Exporting predictions

Once you have predictions on new data, you will need to use them in some fashion, either to send out a mailing or email, place them in a database so they can be accessed with other tools, or create a report on the predictions. In many instances, you may want to export the results as a data file to another format. Modeler has several types of file exports, and these can be seen in the **Export** Palette.

As a side note, it is also very common to export once you have completed data preparation. This allows you to simplify and streamline the use of Modeler so that you do not have to rerun the stream(s), but just open the data file and proceed to modeling.

In this example, we will export the predictions using the **Flat File** Export node. This node allows you to export all or some fields including model predictions to a program such as Notepad:

1. Add a **Flat File** export node to the stream.
2. Connect the generated model to the **Flat File** node.
3. Edit the **Flat File** node.

Data written to a flat file can be read by a variety of other software. You can even use word-processing software to read or edit these files, since they are simple text. You have choices to overwrite an existing file of the same name, or to append it to the existing file. The file name will be given no extension, but you may want to add the a `.dat` or `.txt` extension to remind you of the file type. Field names will be written to the first row of the data file.

The **Field separator** is a **Comma**, but you can change that to any convenient character. Symbolic fields have double quotes placed around their values, and this can be altered if you prefer.

Conveniently, since you may well plan to read the file into Modeler later for modeling, Modeler will generate an import node you can use for this purpose (**Generate an import node for this data** checkbox).

To export the predictions:

1. Change the **Export file** name to `Predictions`.
2. Change the directory location to whatever is convenient.

3. Click **Save:**

4. Click **Run.**

The file has now been exported and you can see these predictions outside of Modeler.

When a model is finally deployed, it is critical that statistics be maintained of the model's accuracy. It is important to establish criteria in advance for assessing model performance, rather than constructing them after first seeing some results. This is partly to get buy-in from key players and groups within the organization. There should be agreement on what constitutes a successful data mining project.

Remember that eventually all models, no matter how accurate they are, will be replaced, so keeping track of model performance will hopefully give you clues about what changes should be made when developing the next generation of models.

Summary

This chapter discussed different ways of assessing the results of a model by using the **Analysis** and **Evaluation** nodes. You also began to learn how to use your models in the real world by learning how to score new data and how to export those predictions.

Index

www.ingramcontent.com/pod-product-compliance
Lightning Source LLC
Chambersburg PA
CBHW080639060326
40690CB00021B/4995